# Mono Lake Viewpoint

Artemisia Press, P. O. box 119, Lee Vining, CA 93541

# Mono Lake Viewpoint
## by
## David Carle

## Illustrated
## by
## Carl Dennis Buell

Artemisia Press, Lee Vining, CA 1992

# Acknowledgements

Without the support of the publisher and editorial staff of the *Mammoth Times* these essays would never have been written, let alone published as a collection. I am grateful to Wally Hofmann for placing my words before the public, and to Mike Jarvis, Scott Weldon and David Strumsky for their gentle editorial touch.

Lauren, Meredith, Carolyn, Patricia, Gary and Susan— the *Writers of the Mono Basin* who've stayed the course— thanks for your critiques and encouragement. W.O.M.B. only works as an acronym for our group if we ignore the "the," but you *have* been a nurturing womb for many of these essays and for my writing in general.

Writers love feedback from readers, and Sally Gaines has always been my most reliable "fan." Publishing this collection has to be the ultimate positive feedback.

The illustrations by Carl Dennis Buell are the perfect complement to this text. Carl has an enormous talent.

Nick and Ryan...you are my inspiration. May the world remain a beautiful place for you and your children.

And Janet. My partner in it all. Thank you, always.

Thank you, all.

# Contents

BEGINNINGS ........................ 7
Beginnings                                    8
Mono Lake Gourmet                            10
A Star Is Born                               14
Tufa Thoughts                                19
SPRING .................................. 23
Is It Spring Yet?                            24
Flies Of Fancy                               28
The Once And Future Shrimp                   32
The Annual Invasion Of Mono Lake             37
The Natural History Of The Easter Bunny      42
What's Biting You?                           47
SUMMER ............................... 51
The Longest Day                              52
A Love Story                                 56
The Phalarope                                61
Take A Tour                                  65
Tsk Tsk Tamarisk                             69
A Summer Gathering And A Woman Scorned       73
AUTUMN ............................... 77
Falling!                                     78
The Mystery Of The Red-eyed Bird             82
Noses, Roses And Roots                       86
Drought Dreams                               90
WINTER ............................... 93
Happy Quiet                                  94
Pogonip                                      97
Ouzel Omens                                 100
Some Winter Voices                          104
IN SEARCH OF HAPPILY EVER AFTER ....... 109
Drain It And Pave It                        110
Money Talk$                                 113
In Search Of Happily Ever After             117
Ten Years Later                             122

Beginnings

# BEGINNINGS

It was cold and windy when we pulled off Highway 395 into the Mono Lake viewpoint on Conway Summit that morning in 1982. Far below us the lake looked gray, filling the basin for mile after mile, but with a tell-tale white bathtub ring circling the shore to the east. My wife, Janet, and I shivered as we studied the view. When a dark cloud began to drop snow onto us we looked at each other in disbelief. We hustled back into the car, wondering if this was typical weather for April. Wondering if we had made the right choice in coming here.

The Mono Lake Tufa State Reserve had been created by the California State Legislature in November, 1981. Janet and I were to fill the one permanent ranger position at the new unit; the first state park rangers in the system to job-share. It was a special opportunity, one that would allow us to start a family while continuing our careers, each working half-time.But that spring morning we had our doubts. The weather was a shock. We would come to know that weather is one of the least predictable things about Mono Lake. We had lots of other lessons to learn as well.

Many first time visitors to Mono Lake feel like they have reached a distant, austere, very strange place. Once they have stopped, explored, taken a close look at the South Tufa area or the north shore below the Mono Lake County Park, those feelings change. The lake's beauty and abundance of life capture most of us, leave us in awe, show us that Mono is the very opposite of a dead sea. Yet this place never looses its strangeness—Mono Lake is something unique.

Most of these essays appeared in the *Mammoth Times* news magazine in 1990 and 1991. This is not a guidebook (several excellent ones are already available on the Mono Lake area.) Many of these essays do not fit the mold of traditional nature writing.

Yet I set out to inform. Environmental education is part of my job as a ranger, after all. It's just more fun to learn about brine shrimp from Merlin the wizard, in "The Once And Future Shrimp," to take one example.

Many of these essays are conversations—dialogue between someone with questions and some other one with answers. Perhaps that comes from my daily experiences at the lake. Park rangers are in the question-and-answer business.

If you are new to Mono Lake, study the table of contents. The essays will introduce you to things which can be found here at any time, and those which are unique to the four seasons.

Mono Lake has been emmeshed in controversy for many years. Decisions made by the courts in 1990 and '91 have us hopeful that the water issue is nearly resolved— that Mono Lake will be stabilized at an elevation where it remains alive and beautiful. There are lessons to be learned from  that fight by involved citizens to save this lake. Perhaps that is my ultimate goal in these stories and essays.

I hope that this book will encourage you to go see for yourself this glorious lake basin that Janet and I learned to love—weather and all.

# MONO LAKE GOURMET

"**G**ood morning! We have two very unusual recipes for today's program, so grab your measuring cups and spoons and prepare to make: "Mock Mono Lake Soup" and "Tufa Porridge Extraordinaire.' Sounds yummy? As always, we offer only the unique and highly seasoned on the *Mono Lake Recipes Show.*

"Ingredients! Mock Mono Lake Soup can be made with normal items you keep around the house, but I'll list the ingredients slowly to give you time to gather them together. Some of these things are not generally kept in the kitchen. Mono Lake has been busily accumulating its various ingredients for over 700,000 years, we figure, so speed is obviously not of the essence.

"Oh, yes, you'll need some sort of closed container. Something that will hold the ingredients in place, creating the perfect environment for a highly seasoned soup. No sieves, you understand. The Mono Basin has no outlet; neither should your bowl.

"So, those ingredients: as you see, we have fresh clean water, direct from the tap. And regular old table salt (sodium chloride, to you chemistry buffs). Then some baking soda; this is very critical to both recipes we are preparing. Do you recall its chemical name, "sodium bicarbonate?" Yes, it is that bitter stuff that helps you burp and feel better when your tummy's upset. Mono Lake is loaded with baking soda. And then, some epsom salts (magnesium sulfate, that is), along with a little borax. Finally, just a pinch of a phosphate-containing laundry soap.

"Ah, your mouth starts to water, no? The key to this recipe is mixing the various ingredients in their correct proportions. Sure, other lakes contain similar minerals, but Mono has its own unique mix of these ingredients. (Perhaps sometime we'll feature a Great Salt Lake recipe, although, personally, I find a certain subtlety lacking in that particular saline soup).

"Here is our first recipe:

Mock Mono Lake Soup
1 quart fresh water
2 ½ Tb salt (chloride)
4 ½ Tb baking soda (carbonate)
2 tsp epsom salts (sulfate)
pinch of borax
pinch of detergent (phosphate)

"Mix well. Exactly how you bring everything together is not important. Mono Lake uses streams, wind, and volcanoes to stir. Eruptions every 500 years or so, thoughout most of the lake's history, have contributed much to the special character and bouquet of Mono Lake's soup.

"To check for 'doneness' rub a little of the soup between your fingers. It should feel slippery. Go on, lick off those wet fingers. Savor the essence of the three primary 'salts,' the chloride, carbonate, and sulfate, mixed in just the right proportions.

"What can you do with this soup? You might try washing your hair. Really! At one time the salts from Mono

Lake were commercially evaporated and packaged for just that purpose. There are some who say that a soak in the water will ease arthritis, but I'm no doctor. If you want to try soaking, rather than mixing up a bathtub-sized batch, you might just come to Mono Lake when it's warm and go for a swim. You'll float like a bobbing cork; all those chemicals dissolved in the water will hold you up. Careful! It will sting if you get the water in your eyes. This is the best way to appreciate the special qualities required of trillions of critters that live their lives in the lake—the brine shrimp, alkali flies, and birds.

"One of the best ways to cap off the experience is to take a freshwater shower after your swim. You will discover that the soapy quality (remember the baking soda, borax and detergent?) really works. Not lots of lather, although waves in the lake often produce mounds of white soapsuds along the beach, but you will get clean and your hair, especially, will end up mysteriously conditioned—soft and easy to comb. (Not that you'd want to shampoo daily in the lake, unless your scalp is so oily that you produce Exxon-size slicks in the water when you bathe.)

"But now, on to our second featured recipe: 'Tufa Porridge Extraordinaire.' This is built around our first concoction, but you'll also need an ingredient that is rarer in most households—calcium chloride. To dissolve properly it should be in a granular or powder form, most often available from chemical supply houses. If you have none handy, just watch closely. My hope is that, after seeing this, you will be motivated to track down the correct stuff. As I always say, a properly stocked spice cabinet is a must if you are going to cook the Mono Lake way.

"So! We mix 2 teaspoons of calcium in a pint of fresh water. That is not a highly concentrated solution, but neither are the springs that come up under Mono Lake. And then, the moment of truth. I now pour the calcium mixture into the Mock Mono Lake Soup, just like a groundwater spring rising up into the lake. Well, not just like—but, what can I say? It is not easy to mimic the way the lake brings the two water solutions together. So we will just pour them together, like so.

"Voila! Look! See it? As soon as the two waters meet, white solid stuff forms. Solid tufa from the mixing of waters! Amazing! I know, I know, it does not look very solid. That is why the recipe is called 'Tufa Porridge.' But if you let it sit awhile, all the solid white calcium carbonate, or tufa, will settle to the bottom of the bowl.

"Should you taste it? Well, actually, this extraordinary porridge is best enjoyed for its decorative qualities—just like the photogenic tufa towers of Mono Lake.

"What's that question? Why did we not form a tufa *tower*? Good, audience! It is because we stirred the waters as we mixed them. But under Mono Lake the little tufa crystals can securely anchor themselves to the bottom, where a spring emerges. And then more crystals hook onto those first ones as the spring keeps flowing. Over time, if conditions are just right, a big tower, as much as 50 feet tall, might grow there. The spring will continue to flow around and up through the building tower. Of course, once the tower reaches the top of the lake it can grow no more. As you now know, the tufa tower must have both Mono Lake, with its carbonates, and fresh springwater with calcium, to make the reaction work.

"And that is our program for today. Thank you for joining me for more unique recipes from that incredible place, Mono Lake. Be with us next time, when we will prepare 'Brine Shrimp Louie' and 'Alkali Fly Pupa Popcorn.' Enjoy!"

# A STAR IS BORN

The star of a show, the one who receives all the attention, may modestly try to make the public see that his performance is only possible because of the combined efforts of a whole team of actors, technicians, producers and directors. But the public seldom buys that message. They want celebrities.

At Mono Lake the celebrity has been the California gull. Since 1979, when the declining lake connected the main gull-nesting island to the shore, the media and the public have focused attention on the plight of the gulls at the Mono Lake. We heard about the abandonment of Negit Island when coyotes crossed the landbridge. We followed the gull colony's numbers: 50,000 adults, raising 30,000 chicks in good years—but the years immediately after the landbridge formed were not so good. During wet years, when the lake rose, the gulls made news again when some nests were re-established on Negit Island. But the drought made that only a temporary return as the landbridge reformed.

The gulls have become the symbol of the lake, the stars of the show.

Yet they could not do their thing here without the support of a cast, crew and production team.

******

By late winter the first flocks of California gulls already begin to arrive in the Mono Basin. They spend the fall and winter on the coast, from Baja California to Oregon. Yet 90% of the California gulls found in this state are born here, on the islands in Mono Lake.

Many people are surprised to find gulls so far inland. Yet this species of gull prefers inland nesting sites with abundant food. Islands are of critical importance, where their nests can be safe from coyotes or other predators that might otherwise walk up and eat their eggs and chicks.

In the spring gulls share lunch with the kids at Lee Vining Elementary School. That early in the season, when the birds are relocating mates and nest sites, the brine shrimp and alkali fly food sources are not yet available in big numbers. By summer the lake will be teeming with enormous quantities of bird food—it will become one massive shrimp soup. But until then the gulls scrounge the dumps and picnic areas, spread out across the region from Bridgeport to Bishop, and every day appear, on schedule when the bell rings to announce lunchtime at the elementary school.

Every day I talk to people about the gulls. Visitors are interested in their status, amazed by their numbers and habits, and, occasionally, mystified about all the hubbub over "some, fer gosh sakes, lousy sea gulls."

Some people apparently go through this thought process:

A. Gulls are the "stars of the show" at Mono Lake.
B. I don't much care about sea gulls, tell you the truth.
C. So why should I care what happens to Mono Lake?

Well. This kind of stuff keeps a ranger's job interesting and challenging.

But where should my response begin? With the facts that will convince that logician that gulls are special, especially the California gull species found here? Or should I leap to the heart of the matter, the real fallacy, as far as I'm concerned? I mean the mistake of the celebrity, star-system approach to looking at things; the charisma method for valuing politicians, movie stars and, yes, ecosystems.

******

It is June. Two speckled eggs, about the size of a chicken's egg, have been carefully guarded and brooded by the gull parents. The scene on the islands is noisy and crowded. Think about the sounds you have heard gulls make. Now imagine thousands of birds packed into a small area. Gray and white avian shapes with black wingtips argue and heckle and cackle and shriek. Figures come and go, hover overhead, then fly off. Since it is June, eggs are hatching throughout the nesting islands. Fluffy, tiny chicks, speckled brown and black, emerge.

Then begins the amazing growth. Parents make trips onto the lake, fill their bellies with shrimp, and return. The hungry chicks peck at red spots on their parents' beaks, and receive gratifying responses. The parents' stomach contents are regurgitated directly into the chicks' open mouths.

And most of them thrive. By mid-July the little balls of fluff will grow to be as big as their parents. But you can easily tell them apart, because when the immature gulls' feathers grow in they appear light brown, all over. They won't develop the distinctive white/gray/black pattern for four years, when they will be adults.

******

Late August. From now on we will see fewer and fewer gulls at the lake every day. They are leaving for the coast. I wonder what it is like for the immature gulls making that first trip across the Sierra. Since the birds are gregarious flock-travelers they will have experienced guides to show them the way. But do you suppose it is something like the first day of school for kindergarteners? Excitement tinged with fear of the unknown?

They'll cross the mountains, then the Central Valley, and eventually reach that *big* lake we call the Pacific Ocean. Less than half as salty as Mono Lake. With other kinds of gulls, and fish, and fishing boats to follow, and maybe a coastal elementary school to visit every day at lunchtime.

For the immature gulls, three or four years will pass before they return to Mono Lake. By then they will be adults, ready to find a mate and locate a choice spot for a nest on one of the islands.

The mature birds will return in the late winter and early spring. Banding studies have shown that a male and female will generally relocate each other, every year, and if possible, will return to the same nest-site.

What if, one year, the gulls came flying over the mountains to discover a changed Mono Lake? What if their "shrimp soup" provided no shrimp? What if the lake shrank so far that no islands were available for safe nesting?

Those "what ifs" are behind the media focus on California gulls in the issues affecting Mono Lake. The gulls are the "stars of the show." But you cannot find proper answers to those questions until you understand the whole picture. Gulls survive here because of their supporting cast and crew. Mono Lake has a unique, harsh chemical-mix of water which supports astonishing amounts of life. Algae becomes food for brine shrimp and fly larvae which are then fed on by birds. That food chain makes it all possible, and if a critical link is severed, the whole production could fail.

50,000 gulls are outnumbered by 140,000 phalaropes and 800,000 eared grebes. Close to 100 species of birds use the lake each year.

None of it stands alone.

People are part of the picture too. We come to the lake to appreciate the beauty of its landscape and setting. We marvel at its wildlife, including the gulls. And we debate, in courts and the legislature, how to resolve conflicts created by human use of the freshwater streams that have always replaced evaporation from Mono Lake.

None of it stands alone. Let's hear it for the gulls. But they couldn't be here if it weren't for a healthy Mono Lake ecosystem, in all its complexity. Long may they be stars in that show.

# TUFA THOUGHTS

A picture is worth a thousand words, but the real thing is always worth a thousand pictures. Even when the subject is as photogenic as tufa.

What's a tufa? First of all, the word is pronounced: "too-faw." Not "tuff-a"—that's a volcanic mineral. Nor "tofu"—the food made from soybean curd.

As a ranger at the Mono Lake Tufa State Reserve, tufa is my main topic—the primary justification for the presence of state park rangers around the shores of Mono Lake. Yet I wrote these articles for the *Mammoth Times* for 18 months before finally tackling the subject of the towers, because words strain to do them justice.

Photographers try to capture their beauty and mystery. In fact, every summer sunrise and sunset brings a mini-rush hour of photographers to the South Tufa area at Mono Lake. But nothing can match being there yourself. You have to see them to believe them.

Plenty of words have been written, of course. The lake's towers have been called "cemented cauliflower," "inferior mortar, dried hard,;" "the skeletons of a dying lake," and "petrified springs." The walk through South Tufa provokes comparisons to a lunar landscape. People struggle to find words to capture the experience and the images.

You need to go see for yourself.

What? You're still sitting there reading? Well, despite the difficulty of the task, I'll have to try words of my own. Maybe a couple more paragraphs will convince you to get up and go.

Think of stalagmites—columns and spires growing up from the floor of a cave below ceiling drips. Now, subtract the cave.

No, that doesn't quite do the job, does it? Cave formations and tufa do have a common chemistry—they are both calcium carbonate. But if you ask a geologist to define "tufa" he should tell you that it is calcium carbonate formed from the mixing of waters. Two water sources are necessary.

Mono Lake's alkaline water provides the carbonates which go into the mix. It is basically just dissolved baking soda. And freshwater, emerging as springs from beneath the lake, provides the calcium source. Mix them together under the right conditions and, *voila*, tufa.

Let the reaction continue for awhile, with the spring flowing constantly up through the heavier, more dense, saltwater. As it rises through and around the growing mass more and more solid material will be deposited. Ultimately, the towers can grow upward until they reach the surface of the lake.

Got that? You can now dazzle your friends with these two fundamental facts: wherever you find a tufa formation, 1) Mono Lake had to have covered that area at some time, and 2) a source of freshwater also had to be present.

Today we walk among many of the towers stranded on dry land. That "petrified springs" image evokes a feeling for the change that has occurred. Few of the tufas stranded on land have springs still gushing through or around them. As Mono Lake dropped (a result of diversion of the streams which once replaced evaporation from the lake), the springs tended to follow the declining shoreline.

Snorkel or scuba dive among the tufas still underwater and you will experience something very different. Many of the underwater towers still appear to have tendrils of fresh-water rising from their peaks. New calcium carbonate crystals can be seen forming. The towers are changing and alive—alive with algae and feasting fly larvae and adult flies walking around in their silver bubbles of air.

The interaction between water and tufa shows up even on land. Visitors to the "groves" don't spend much of their time amidst the dry, upland formations. Most of you walk the shoreline itself, where the towers meet the lake and where the best views can be had of towers jutting from the water off-shore (like emerging "skeletons?"), doubled in number and scale by their mirror-image reflections on the lake surface.

It is true that the decline in the lake has actually allowed us to walk among the tufa towers. It is also true that experiencing the tufas, without the lake, is not the same. If you want to see tufa formations in a dry lake you can visit "the pinnacles" in the dry bed of Searles Lake, near Ridgecrest. But that spot doesn't attract close to 200,000 visitors each year.

Mono Lake's tufa formations are the primary focus of the State Reserve. But they are just part of an unusual mix of scenery, setting and life at Mono Lake. The total package is what impresses most; something more than the sum of its individual parts.

It took me this long to finally write about tufa because they are not easy to capture in words. But most of all because they are only part of the whole.

Come and see for yourself. Bring your camera. You will find yourself looking far across the lake, at the vista of the Sierra crest to the west and volcanic formations forming the other three walls of the basin. Soon your focus will shift. Textures and color and light will vary and change. A flock of birds will suddenly come into the picture. And as your attention moves in closer and closer, you will become aware that the water near your feet teems with life—brine shrimp and alkali flies, the unique animals adapted to this unique chemical soup.

Bent over now, peering into the water, you may suddenly spot a freshwater spring, not mixing with the salty lakewater, but pushing up through in its quest to float atop the brine. And there, around the base of the spring, you may see yellowish crystals of calcium carbonate being added to the rocky bottom.

The water of Mono Lake is at the center of it all. Salty, soapy, and strange. It controls what can—and cannot—live here. It is at the center of human controversy over this lake. And it creates the conditions for tufa towers to form.

There's a joke that says that the name "tufa" is used here because people used to sell these decorative towers "tu-fa the price of one." No such sale could ever be held for Mono Lake as a whole. In its beauty, setting, and life, Mono Lake is one of a kind.

You need to go see for yourself.

Spring

# IS IT SPRING YET?

*"There are only two seasons in the region round about Mono Lake—and these are, the breaking up of one winter and the beginning of the next."* Mark Twain, *Roughing It*

Oh, balderdash, Mr. Twain. I am afraid you were writing nonsense when you made that statement. Actually, like everywhere else, there are four seasons in our annual deck.

It's just that they somehow get shuffled together, so that the order and length of our seasons are...well, all mixed up. That's why the vernal equinox can be warm and sunny—with birds chirping and green things poking through the damp soil—or it can just as easily produce a bone-numbing blizzard.

So how can you tell it is spring?

It can get confusing. Easter is usually a good sign of spring. But in these parts the Lions Club Easter egg hunt gets postponed occasionally—whenever conditions suggest that the annual event is more likely to become a search for wee little egg hunters lost in the snow drifts.

Officially spring arrives when the lengthening daylight hours finally equal those of nighttime—the equinox. But I tend to focus less on day length and more on warmth. It's not really spring until I can take off my long underwear.

Dressing for the cold, particularly for those of us who work outdoors, is a major factor in the daily routine of mountain residents. With lycra-, polypro- and wool-everything, it's more and more possible to be comfortably functional in winter weather. But it feels so good when I can remove the extra layers, and even expose some skin again. (Not to mention the springtime pleasures of watching other bare skin reappear on public display.) Maybe the essence of spring is bare-skin weather.

Several years ago I was cross-country skiing with some friends on the west shore of Mono Lake in early February. It was one of those winters before the drought, when a whole lot of snow had accumulated in the area. The town of Mammoth Lakes seemed almost buried under six to eight foot drifts. The west shore of Mono Lake had enough snow, two or three feet, to cover the shrubs and make skiing possible. The day was cold, quiet, under a threatening overcast sky. Suddenly all of us stopped skiing and listened. There was a sound, out-of-place, but strangely familiar: the yammering, squawking, high-pitched, celebratory, rowdy calls of the first flock of California gulls returning to Mono Lake for their spring breeding and summer chick-rearing festival.

The gulls sounded excited about coming over the Sierra crest and receiving their first view of the lake. As the flock of 30 birds wheeled off to the northeast, snow began to fall from the dark clouds, like powdered sugar from a sifter.

Despite that reminder that it was still winter, the gulls showed me that change was just around the corner. That long winter really *was* going to reach an end. I felt like squawking my own rowdy defiance at the clouds. So maybe spring begins with the return of birds, whatever the weather suggests to the contrary.

But there are other signs that let you know spring has sprung: the shrinking of the firewood pile out back; crocus bulbs popping up, daring to emerge despite the deck shuffler's habit of dealing us a hard freeze as soon as the flowers open.

Some years the opening of Tioga Pass is when I finally believe that the season has truly arrived. Maybe that's because the road-opening coincides with an increase in the demands of my job as a ranger. When the pass opens, tourists also join the seasonal migration back to the Mono Basin. For many business people around Mono County the opening day of fishing season is a similar herald of spring, for similar reasons. It doesn't work that way for us at Mono Lake, though. Rarely do we run into an optimistic angler with a line in the lake, not realizing that fish just get pickled in this alkaline water.

I know it's spring when Mono Lake is pea soup green again, full of algae not yet harvested by the microscopic, just-hatched brine shrimp. And one of the best indicators, for me, has become the return of the violet-green swallows. Each spring they come back to build nests in the holes of tufa towers. Flashing white breasts, they streak back and forth over our heads, with their muppet-style mouths wide open, ready to scoop in flying insects. By midsummer they have gone again—and that is also about when I realize that spring is long gone too.

Back in 1982, our first summer here, Janet and I were in the ghost town of Bodie State Historic Park, helping prepare a float for the 4th of July parade in Bridgeport. I remember looking out the window of the big barn, just after sunset, and being astonished to see heavy, wet, fluffy snowflakes falling thickly from the sky. It was winter up there, that night in early July. I can hear Mark Twain now, cackling triumphantly, "Aha! My point, exactly. Winter in July; it's always winter in that region."

However, Mark is overlooking what happened the next morning. Shortly after the sun rose, it was spring—that is, until about 11 A.M., when it became summer again. But during those few morning hours, the folks in Bodie experienced a true spring: everything felt clean and new, spirits were refreshed, sap was rising, and, most of all they could take off their long underwear again.

I pity those poor places that only get one spring every year.

# FLIES OF FANCY

He avoids contact with people whenever possible. Disdaining scuba tanks, he is often seen moving around underwater, breathing from air bubbles trapped among his body hairs. He can even walk on water.

Sounds like a particularly talented, but surly, member of the June Lake Mountain Rescue Dive Team, you say? Wrong!

A few more hints: his life immediately prior to adulthood was spent just lying around, appearing lethargic enough to make one wonder whether he would ever amount to anything. But, hey, wasn't that the case for a lot of us, too? Many of his ancestors never made it past that stage of their lives, instead becoming food for the natives who lived in the area. They tasted *good*.

But this one matured; became an adult. His full name is *Ephydra hydropyrus hians*. The middle name means "water fire." Many folks call him a "brine fly," but "alkali fly" is most accurate, according to the scientists.

Yep, a fly. A member of that pesky order of insects that we all love to hate. Why *did* God make flies anyway? Why do they have to bite us, hover around us, make that awful whining buzz, and feed on yucky, putrifying gunk before arriving to trample over our picnic food with their germy feet? All flies are worthless, crummy pests. Right?

Wrong again, I'm afraid. You see, the flies that inhabit Mono Lake are different from most of their obnoxious cousins. Visit the shore of Mono Lake during warm weather and you may encounter a three-foot-wide, black, buzzing band of brine flies blocking your way to the beach. But, never fear, all you need do is approach and they will hurriedly fly away from you. If one happens to bump into your leg, you can be assured it was a mistake. They don't like us. I think *they* consider *people* awful and bothersome (perhaps even yucky).

Their nice behavior may have something to do with an alkali fly's choice of food. They are primarily vegetarians, feasting on algae found along the shore and on the submerged rocks of Mono Lake. So they have no appetite for human meat.

But they do have lots of enemies that are interested in making a meal out of *them*. Birds love them. It's interesting to watch a gull wading along through the crowded mass of flies by the shore, swiping and pecking at the flies. As the bird walks the flies clear out, but they seem to know just how far to go to be out of reach. The result is that the gull looks like it has a force field surrounding it that repels all flies within six inches of its beak.

Of course, now and then, the beak is quicker than the fly.

If there were Olympic games to celebrate the ultimate achievements in alkali fly talents, one of the events would be speed skating. Not on ice, but over the surface of the liquid water. There would have to be other events even less familiar to us. Like underwater rock climbing. The adult flies don't dive and swim when they go underwater to eat and lay eggs. Instead, they walk down, using hooked claws to cling to the tufa rocks. I imagine scoring criteria for this event would include both speed and style: "Incredible! For the first time in history a successful one-claw transfer between tufas has been completed. But he's about out of air now..."

A whole series of events might be built around their ability to breathe underwater by encasing themselves in bubbles of air. Of course, the temptation for alkali fly athletes to boost their bristly body hair density, in order to trap bigger and bigger bubbles of air as they enter the lake, could lead to deplorable abuses of banned substances (whatever the fly equivalent of anabolic steroids might be).

The adolescent larvae athletes could compete in algae scraping contests, crawling over tufa rocks to see who could first fill his belly. Or lime gland weight-lifting, for those who have best refined their ability to handle the carbonates in the alkaline water by mixing it with calcium and storing the resultant tufa-like stuff in an increasingly heavy, glandular pocket.

Even the pupae that appear so outwardly quiet in their brown, coccoon-like cases, could show off their amazing abilities at time-warping. Just how far can the limits be pushed? In one arena flies are vying for the 3-day pupation record; it's hot in there, folks. While over here, two flies are chilled dangerously close to the point of death, attempting to extend their pupa stages to 10 weeks. What is this thing we call time, anyway? Both sets of flies will complete identical portions of their allotted lives, but in vastly different spans, solely dependent on temperature.

Amazing facts, certainly. But who really cares, you ask? They are still only a bunch of flies, after all.

Well, besides the thousands of birds that feast on them, the Kuzedika Paiute Indians cared. They relied on fly pupae as one of the staples of their diets. Our culture's dietary staples are corn and wheat. For the Kuzedika residents of the Mono Basin it was pinyon pinenuts and fly pupae. They called the pupae, "kutsavi," and used it as a supplement to other food or just as a popcorn-style handfood.

Kutsavi was good food. Good in terms of nutrition, but also flavor. In fact, it was a highly valued trade item. Indians from far away coveted Mono Lake's fly pupae.

Which brings us to the word "mono." Did you know the lake is in "Fly Pupae County?" "Mono" is a Yokuts word. The Yokuts Indians lived west of Yosemite, and would hike up into the mountains during the summer to trade with the Yosemite Miwoks and with the Paiutes, who had traveled over the Sierras from the east side. The Yokuts loved "mono," yummy, nicely-seasoned fly pupae from the salty sea across the mountains.

Why don't we call this "Kutsavi Lake" and "Kutsavi County?" Why use a name from people that lived so far away?

Because of the way California was settled, the Anglo culture made contact with the Indians on the west side of the mountains first. One story is that when the lake was officially discovered by a U.S. Cavalry troop chasing Indians eastward from Yosemite, their guides were Yokuts. The guides taught them the name "mono" for this area. And that name is what we still use today: Mono Lake, Mono County, the Mono Cone...

It all goes back to a little fly that has the unique ability to survive in the harsh alkaline waters of Mono Lake.

# THE ONCE AND FUTURE SHRIMP

*In T.H. White's, The Once and Future King, a young boy called Wart—who will grow up to become King Arthur—is tutored by the wizard, Merlin, who lives backwards through time. Merlin, with his talking owl, Archimedes, teaches lessons by turning Wart into various animals.*

"Quiet, boy. This is a difficult spell. Hmm. Let's see. Was it 'Artemus monolus'? No, that's not right. Drat!"

Wart knew better than to interrupt the wizard at a time like this. His spells had a way of going wrong at the best of times. But he could not help asking, "What am I going to become this time? I hope it's something big and fierce. Last time I almost—"

"Shush! I've got it now."

With a wave of his arms and a strange incantation, Merlin and Wart, along with Archimedes the owl, suddenly found themselves in a place that looked very strange to a boy used to England's lush greenery. They were standing on sand, in a vast expanse dotted with greyish shrubs. Directly in front of them a blue lake stretched away for miles, with hundreds of birds swimming on its surface.

"Oh, Archimedes," Wart said, "I don't think we're in England anymore."

The wizard laughed and the owl hooted. "Shades of Dorothy and Toto," Merlin said.

"Who?"

"Oh, never mind. That movie won't be made for centuries yet. We better get on with our business here."

Wart was about to ask what a movie was, but his attention was caught by movement in the lakewater.

"Look! There are little wiggly worms in this water. Gobs of them!"

He dipped his hands into the lake, but the half-inch long creatures slipped away.

"Taste some of the water," Merlin said.

Wart gulped down the water in his scooped palms. And quickly spat it right back out. "Pah!"

Merlin put a hand on Wart's shoulder. "Salty and bitter, isn't it? This is Mono Lake. A long, long way from England; you're right about that. But a good place to learn another lesson. Are you ready?"

"I—I don't know. Not if I'm going to become something that swims in that horrible water."

"Don't judge a place before you understand it." And then Merlin crossed his arms and began to chant. "Artemia monicus, alakazam, brinicus wigglepus, flibbityjam."

Suddenly Wart felt himself shrinking. His backbone turned to jelly. The bones in his body dissolved and he began to grow new limbs: one, two, three...he counted 11 arms on each side before the process stopped. As his head shrank, his eyes grew bigger and bigger. Like some bug-eyed monster, he thought. He found he could see in all directions at once, because his eyes stuck out so far from the sides of his little head. And then he discovered his tail.

It was great! The tail was almost as long as the rest of him put together. When he thrashed it to one side, it made his upper body swing in the opposite direction. It was tricky to move around, coordinating the 22 legs as oars, and the tail as a rudder. He found himself swimming in loop-the-loop circles and then upside down, staring up at the light sparkling on the surface of the water.

It was then that Wart realized that he felt no need to surface and take a breath. And while he was digesting that fact, he also became aware that he was steadily digesting food. He had been constantly swallowing bits of tiny plants as he swam.

"Well, boy, what do you think?"

"Wha—? Merlin, is that you?" Wart looked closely at the feathery-looking creature swimming beside him.

"Hold still, boy, you're making me dizzy watching you. Not that you swim any less crazily than the rest of these brine shrimp."

"Is that what I am?" Now swimming in more of a straight line, Wart noticed that the water all around was crowded with shrimp. "Merlin, what are those couples doing? Is that a dance?"

Merlin chuckled. "You might call it that. Hmmm. You're a bit young for this part of the story. Let's just say that when a male and female brine shrimp, um, get married, they swim around together in a sort of dance, sometimes for days."

"I'm not so very young. I'll bet the round things inside the clear pouches on some of the shrimp are eggs. Right? Those are the lady shrimp, huh?"

"Good deduction, boy. That lady will probably give birth to babies from that pouch soon now. Odd thing is that later this season she'll have more eggs, but she'll just release them to sink to the lake bottom. They'll lay there until next spring before hatching out, all on their own."

"How will the babies find their mothers, then?"

"Never will. Won't need to. In fact, all the shrimp you see here will live their full lives before another spring comes."

They swam together in silence for awhile, until Wart said, "Merlin, we're in Mono Lake now, right? Why doesn't it taste awful anymore?"

"Because you've become a Mono Lake brine shrimp; something unique, even within the illustrious family of shrimps. One of the only creatures on earth that can stand this salty, alkaline—"

"Alkaline? What's that?"

"A solution high in hydroxyl ions, such—"

"Oh, don't confuse the boy." The new voice belonged to Archimedes. Wart looked up and saw the owl gliding above the water surface. He appeared oddly distorted, seen through the water. "'Alkaline' is 'soapy,' Wart. That's all you need to know. You're in a big soapy soup. Not many creatures can stand such water."

"Not many? Why there must be thousands of us just right here close by. And the lake looked enormous. If—"

"I mean not many *kinds* of creatures. In fact, you brine shrimp and some flies are the only animals found in this lake. You can have it too, to my mind. When are we leaving here, Merlin? I'm getting salt-spray in my feathers."

"What's that?" Merlin, asked, absentmindedly. "I wasn't...drat, where'd Wart get too? Archimedes, can you see him?"

"No. There are so many of you swarming around that it's hard to keep track of who's who. Why don't you just use some magic and...WATCH OUT!"

******

Wart had wandered off, following a female shrimp, hoping to find some way to talk to her, when suddenly a dark shadow blocked the sun. He looked toward the surface and saw two giant bird legs kicking through the water. And then the female he had followed was suddenly gone, grasped by an enormous beak. Wart back-pedaled furiously, trying to avoid being caught by that massive beak himself. The bird pecked again and again at the water. Dozens of shrimp disappeared as he watched in horror.

But there was safety in numbers for Wart. Realizing that, he calmed a little. Even though the bird had eaten so many shrimp, the water around him still looked crammed with others. It was as though the loss of a few individual lives meant nothing at all.

Suddenly Wart felt very lonely. It dawned on him that he no longer heard Merlin's voice. He called out, "Merlin! Come get me out of here. It means a lot to *me* if I'm eaten. I want to be a human again. Merlin...!"

******

"Well, you almost did it that time," the owl said, scolding the wizard. Wart looked up at the familiar voice. He was lying on the sandy beach, dripping wet. The wizard, also wet and bedraggled, was wringing out his long beard.

"Oh, blast and be bothered! If that gull hadn't swallowed me whole...do you know how difficult it is to cast a spell from inside a gull's throat?"

"Merlin," Wart said, "I didn't like being just one little shrimp among millions."

"Well then, you learned something. Good! You know, there are more than 'millions' here; about 4 trillion, to be exact. That is 4 followed by 12 zeroes. Yet, oddly, someday people who drive by this lake will look out their car windows and think the whole place looks dead."

"Drive? Car? What—?"

"Never mind. It's time to go. Stand up, Wart. Are you ready?" He crossed his arms, preparing to cast the spell.

"I guess." Wart turned for a last look at the lake. "All those lives," he said quietly. "I wish I could have talked to her."

And then the three visitors disappeared. And the shore of Mono Lake was quiet once again.

# THE ANNUAL INVASION OF MONO LAKE

D*ear Dave, Dave and Janet,*
*I really liked the trip to Mono Lake. But I got sick on the way back to school. I really liked the tufa towers, and I enjoyed watching the gulls. Thank you.*

*Heather Roseter*

Rangers at Mono Lake look forward to this time of year with anticipation tinged with dread. This is the season that fills their jobs with meaning, fills their bodies with fatigue and turns their minds to silly putty.

No, I don't mean summer. That "busy season" pales in comparison. I'm talking about the entire month of May and first two weeks of June. The horrible, wonderful season when school groups mob the shores of Mono Lake.

*Dear Dave, Dave and Janet,*

*I liked Mono Lake and the volcanoes. I liked it when Carly was eating the pupa and she said it tasted like bubble gum! I never tasted it. Thank you, your friend,*

*Remedios*

The school group season is the busiest time of year for the rangers at the Mono Lake Tufa State Reserve. Every day we have several school groups visiting the lake. We generally take them on a one-and-a-half hour guided walk, exploring the lakeshore. This year, 1991, the Reserve will conduct tours for Crowley Christian School, Truckee Elementary, the Bridgeport preschool, six classes from Pine Street School in Bishop, four classes from Babbitt Elementary in Hawthorne, Nevada, the Schurz School of Nevada, Kings Beach Elementary from Tahoe, the entire student body of Beamon Elementary, a class from Lone Pine, one from Carson City, one from the Central Valley town of Fellows, and even for the local Lee Vining Elementary first and second graders.

Then we'll collapse into the relative calm of our summer busy season.

*Dear Janet,*

*Thank you for touring us around. I learned a lot. My friend Janett, her braun [sic] shrimp had a baby. Isn't that great? Thanks for letting us look in your bonoculars [sic]. I had fun. Got to go. Bye.*

*Kristiana Kliks*

Do you remember how you felt about field trips when you were in school? The excitement about going somewhere special and getting out of the same old routine? If you went someplace outdoors, your teacher probably scheduled the trip in the spring, shortly before the school year ended.

Of course, spring is when the weather is most reliable. But there's no denying that field trips also help channel the energy of kids who are unbearably excited about the approach of summer vacation. Every so often we rangers get the impression that the trip is just a chance for a teacher to reward her kids and herself with a well-earned fun outing—payback for tolerating each other throughout the school year. Fortunately, most of the classes don't descend upon us with such a casual attitude.

More often the teachers have worked to prepare the kids. They view our efforts as a helpful adjunct to their curriculum. We like to think that attitude is no accident. We have worked to build a reputation as environmental education professionals (one of the many "hats" that park rangers wear in their jobs these days). We encourage pre- and post-instruction on the concepts learned at Mono Lake. Every teacher from Bridgeport to Bishop has been provided a copy of the *Teacher's Guide to Mono Lake and the Mono Basin*, courtesy of the Sierra State Parks Foundation. Most importantly, we conduct our tours with a specific set of objectives, hoping the kids go back with more than just a bunch of unrelated facts.

Our big advantage over the classroom setting is that we get to deal with real stuff: slippery, wiggly, cold, smelly, pretty, dainty, gross, yucky, living stuff. It's fun. Our challenge is to shape that experience into something educational, in a way that will stick with the kids.

*Dear Dave,*

*As you can see from these letters my class truly enjoyed their Mono Lake adventure! The program that Janet gave really served to prepare them for tours that followed at the lake. On the tour the high point had to be eating the pupae. What a clever trick you used to get us to try them. That afternoon, many of the children had a Little League game. All of the parents reported that the children talked constantly about the trip all the way to Gardner-ville. It was a wonderful experience. Thank you so much. Sincerely,*

*Robin Hook, 2nd grade teacher, Antelope Elementary*

With such lofty goals, we often wonder how we are doing. Does any of it really matter? What about those kids who we couldn't seem to grab, the ones that kept wandering away from the group? It's small consolation, when you think you've failed with one, to hear from the teacher that that child is her "problem" every day. So I've learned to ask teachers, before we start walking, to identify those predictably difficult kids. Those are the ones I involve first, getting their help with demonstrations, carrying or holding something—trying to win them over.

Sometimes, with certain kids, we clearly fail. Then we can only hope that the place itself will work its magic, impressing the student with the lessons that are there for everyone to learn, teacher or ranger notwithstanding.

We love it when a class writes us letters. Especially when they tell us specific things that they liked or learned. We get immediate feedback too, of course. Recently Janet had an eighth grade class at the lake. As always she gave them the chance to eat a few brine fly pupae. It's not as though they can really taste Kutsavi as prepared by the local Indians, but it builds a memory. Once you've bravely eaten one, you will always remember: a) that brine flies exist; b) that this fly is important to people and birds at this lake; and c) that different cultures solve the problem of food in different ways. Well, as that group walked along after tasting some pupae, one girl gushed, "I, like, can't believe I ate a *bug*! I'm normally so clean; I just don't *do* things like that! It's *totally* ruined my reputation!"

I *think* we won in that encounter. *Like, totally.* We keep on trying, anyway, because it's important—one of the most important roles that comes with the ranger job.

In the midst of field trip fun we hope to send students home with an appreciation for the unique features of Mono Lake. But much broader than that, we hope that the lake will teach universal lessons about food chains and ecosystems and about the ways that living things, including humans, are interdependent.

We hope they will go away understanding why John Muir wrote, "When we try to pick out anything by itself we find it hitched to everything else in the universe."

Heavy stuff, coated in a sugar pill of fun.

*Dear Dave, Dave and Janet,*

*It was fun catching brine shrimp. I like the tufa towers and the volcanoes. I thank you for a good time, rangers.*

*Clay Sowders*

# A NATURAL HISTORY OF THE EASTER BUNNY

If you've ever wondered about the Easter Bunny, I've got a theory that explains: I. Who he (or she—do you really know for sure?) is, and II. Why he (or she—heck, I'm just going to shorten this to E.B.) took up egg delivery to children this time of year.

I don't claim to have any inside knowledge about E.B., mind you. I've never interviewed E.B., nor even caught E.B. in the act of hiding the candy eggs that so mysteriously appear around our house and yard each year. But it's my job to watch and learn from the critters I encounter near Mono Lake. And the evidence is piling up.

I. Who is the Easter Bunny?

I believe E.B. is a whitetailed jackrabbit that made the bigtime. This exceptional individual was born somewhere in the western mountains or high plains of North America, some late spring or early summer. E.B. was undoubtedly one of 2 or 3 in a litter, and might have been expected to lead the normal life of a whitetailed jackrabbit: active at late dusk and into the night; rarely seen, secretive; never building a burrow or home, but sheltering among shrubs by day or to wait out winter storms. Each winter its coat would change from mottled brown to white.

Like all whitetails, E.B. is bigger than the other rabbits and hares found in this area. Near Mono Lake we have four members of this family: tiny brush rabbits with short ears and almost no tail; cute little cottontails—slightly bigger; blacktail jackrabbits—much bigger still, with long, long ears—they are the ones most commonly noticed by people near the lake; and the whitetail jacks, rarest and largest. They can weigh up to 10 pounds and stand 20 inches tall, not counting their six-inch-long ears.

I've only seen two whitetails in ten years at Mono Lake. If I spent more time wandering around after dark undoubtedly I'd run across more. But they *are* somewhat rare.

My closest encounter was in broad daylight, on the north shore of Mono Lake, last summer. I was on foot, walking across the white glare of a salt encrusted cobble beach. I turned to see what had moved in the corner of my vision. Nothing. I walked slowly ahead, still looking over that way. And the rabbit hopped forward a few steps too, not thirty feet away. Its motion gave it away.

Now we stared at each other. I have no idea what it was thinking, but *my* reaction was, "What a giant!" The extrordinary size was the clue that made me check the tail color. Yep. It wasn't black, like most of the jacks we see. A real live whitetail. The only other I'd ever seen was speeding across the highway one night, caught by my headlights.

The books say these guys can run up to 40 miles per hour and make leaps of 17 feet. But at the moment this one was trying to pretend it was invisible. Sure, I was staring its direction, but maybe the frozen-critter tactic would still work. That's their first strategy, generally. Don't move. Blend into the scenery while the potential predator walks on past. Save the speed for the last minute, then let them eat your dust. Streak on out, zig-zagging, then throw in a couple big upward leaps so you can glance back and keep track of the pursuit.

This one didn't run. I took a few slow steps closer, wishing I had binoculars. It kept its distance with a few slow steps of its own, away.

Now I have something a bit strange to confess. This rabbit began to make me nervous. Its stare seemed to say, "I'm not going to back down to you, little human." I mean, this was a BIG rabbit, and it was just the two of us on that beach. It seemed wary, but not intimidated, if you follow me.

If I was hungry and inclined that way, it could've made a meal for my whole family. It should've been scared. It wasn't to know that the only thing I wished I could shoot it with was a camera.

Yet it stared me down. "Don't mess with me, sucker," was the message. "I'm strong and fast and a survivor, hear?"

Well, eventually the impasse was broken. It hobbled a few more steps until it was out of sight over a rise. And when I walked to the top of that rise, it had disappeared completely.

Mysterious. Rare. Doesn't that sound like a good candidate for E.B.?

II. Why does E.B. hide eggs?

Come to the South Tufa area at Mono Lake sometime soon. Come to see the tufa towers and brine shrimp and birds and gorgeous scenery, of course. But while you're there, take a short side-trip out among the shrubs. You might spook a rabbit from its daytime shelter, but even if you don't see one, you can't miss the clear evidence of their presence.

Every shrub has been pruned up about twenty inches from the ground. And around the base of each plant is an amazing quantity of little round "gifts."

Small, dark pellet-droppings are sometimes left by the cottontails. But the marble-sized, vegetable-matter pellets of the jackrabbits are ubiquitous.

They are so big and so numerous that visitors sometimes doubt my explanation about their origins. They think it must have all come from larger animals—deer, or something. People who are used to seeing domestic rabbits or cottontails have trouble grasping how much larger a jackrabbit is than its cousins.

The early settlers in the West named them "Jack-Ass Rabbits," because of their donkey-long ears. Got shortened to jackrabbit, of course. They were important in the diet of the local Indians, who also twisted and wove the warm fur into wonderful blankets. The jackrabbit is a western fixture that tends to be overlooked when humans choose symbols to idolize. We focus on buffalo and grizzlys and wolves and eagles. Jackrabbits aren't glamorous. Just successful.

Those accumulations around the bushes are there because that's where the rabbits spend so much time. Jackrabbits are technically "hares." Unlike "rabbits," they never dig burrows and their babies are born under some shrub. At birth the babes already have fur. By contrast, rabbits like cottontails—and Bugs Bunny—shelter in holes and give birth to "naked," more helpless, young.

Inevitably, hanging out in the shrubs for cover and for food, their droppings accumulate. Jacks seem to really be concentrated near South Tufa, especially in the winter. The snow is not so deep there, for one thing, but the big attraction is the "food pantry." The shrub that has most successfully invaded the exposed bottom of Mono Lake, with its salty soil, is called "rabbitbrush." It's the shrub that produces yellow flowers in the late summer. Its stems remain succulent in the winter when most other bushes are less edible.

And around each rabbitbrush bush, the rabbits leave behind "presents." That is truly the impression you'll have when you see the phenomenon at South Tufa.

So imagine a hare—a great big, secretive, whitetailed jackrabbit—who zips around at night leaving piles of "jellybean" sized pellets in the natural hiding places afforded by each shrub. And imagine some exceptional individual whitetail, once upon a time, that took its natural abilities and inclinitions to the next logical step.

I submit, the evidence—though circumstantial—is compelling.

The Easter Bunny is a whitetail jackrabbit. Now you know.

# WHAT'S BITING YOU?

**"S**o what's bugging you?"

"That's *my* question. I've got itchy little red spots and some sort of tiny gnats keep whining around my head. What are they?"

"A sure sign that it's May or June in the Mono Basin. They're called no-see-ums. Found in lots of desert-type places with alkaline ponds or lakes."

"You don't mean Mono Lake produces these things? No. Say it isn't so. Mono Lake has always seemed so special, so beautiful. But this could change my whole attitude about the place. These no-see-ums are a drag."

"Sorry. It's true. Their larvae live in the lakewater."

"Are you sure? It seems like they're worse in the sagebrush away from the lake."

"Even though the midges are tiny, they can move around the Basin. If the lakeshore has less of a problem it's probably because it's windy there so much of the time. Even a light breeze keeps the no-see-ums from bothering folks."

"What I want to know is what they do for food when they can't get humans?"

"Oh, any mammal will do. Did you know it is only the females that have such fierce biting habits?"

"Ha! So my innate attractiveness to females is the problem, eh?"

"Don't take it so personally. They love all us humans."

"Another thing that puzzles me is why they love our hair. Drives me crazy."

"Who knows? Probably it's a nice cozy shelter, down among all the hairs, away from the wind. I imagine if you're a no-see-um the wind is your biggest gripe about the way the planet was created. Can't you just hear the little buzzers saying, 'Why did God have to make wind, anyway? Pushing us around all the time. Oh, well, fellow midges, let's just be thankful He provided so many mammals, chock full of blood, with nice thick hair in which to shelter."

"Yeah, and with ears to crawl down into."

"Ooh, I know, don't you hate that? They get inside, humming away, and there's nothing you can do. You'd think they would just head for the light and find their way back out."

"So, you're not thrilled about them either. But I notice they're not bothering you now. How come?"

"Oh, folks around here have figured out that a certain bath oil, which leaves your skin so soft when used in the tub, can be applied directly onto skin. It makes no-see-ums gag. Well, it repels them, anyway."

"Aren't no-see-ums relatives of the brine flies at Mono Lake? *They* don't bother people this way."

"True. The brine flies are the shy flies. The no-see-ums are flies, but in a different family: Ceratopogonidae. Also known as punkies, midges, gnats or sand flies. Only a couple millimeters long, but with bites all out of proportion to their size."

"I consider myself an environmentalist and I know that everything has a role to play in the ecosystem. Still, I can't help wondering—"

"Why God made wind?"

"No, that's the no-see-ums' question. I want to know—"

"Why the peak of the no-see-um season lasts only about 6 weeks?"

"No, that wasn't it either. Any length season is too long, in my opinion. But tell me—"

"Why the Mono Lake area isn't blessed with pesky mosquitoes, like so much of the rest of Mono County?"

"You know, now that you mention it, that's true. But I bet I can explain that myself. There's not a lot of standing freshwater around the lake. I guess Mono Lake itself is too salty, or something, for mosquitoes, huh? So they aren't around here, not like in the alpine, highcountry meadows."

"Right. But no-see-ums just love salty, alkaline water. In fact, as the lake has shrunk, becoming more salty, conditions may have actually improved for the no-see-ums. That's just speculation, you understand, But I interrupted you earlier, several times, in fact. You couldn't help wondering...?"

Thoughtful silence. A sigh. Sudden furious scratching of a head.

"Aargh! I'm sorry, but I've *got* to get out of here."

Starts to leave, then turns around and says, "Look, I know what you were trying to tell me with all your interruptions. I guess I can still appreciate the wonders of Mono Lake, even though it also produces no-see-ums."

"Hooray! As Mark Twain wrote after he visited here, 'Everything has its part and proper place in nature's economy.' And as John Muir wrote, 'When we try to pick out anything by itself, we find it hitched to everything else in the universe.' And as—"

"Stop! I hear you. Everything has its part to play. Even no-see-ums...and their human blood donors." A laugh while swatting at the air. "Donating to help the Mono Lake ecosystem has suddenly taken on a whole new perspective for me."

Summer

# THE LONGEST DAY

 **S**ummer officially began today. This is the summer solstice—the day the sun climbs highest into the sky for those of us living in the northern hemisphere.

As this tilted planet moves in its orbit around the sun, eventually leaning our portion of the globe toward the big solar power source, the days last longer and more energy makes it through the atmosphere. You might think that the longest day would coincide with the hottest, driest, most August-like weather. Doesn't work that way. It takes awhile—there's a lag—before the lengthening days translate their energy to our weather patterns.

Summer is the time of leisurely twilight hours. It's impossible to get kids in bed at their normal time, but, after all, school is out. It's time to sit outside on warm evenings, watching charcoal glow in the barbecue, day-glow fade over the Sierra crest and alpenglow turn the White Mountains pink.

The signs of summer are clear. This time every year, someone opens a gate somewhere and lets the motorhomes and travel-trailers loose. All of a sudden you have to add fifteen minutes to the estimated driving time from Mono

Lake to Mammoth. I can live with that, but not with the frustrated, crazy drivers who start passing on curves and hills; summer is head-on-collision and near-miss season, too. So use those turn-outs, *please*, slow-rig-drivers, whenever a line of cars is behind you.

This time every year, someone opens a gate somewhere and lets the CalTrans workers loose. They only have so many weeks in this part of the world to get their repairs done. It's unfortunate that the road-work season coincides with the summer travel season. So add another lump of time to get anywhere—and give the folks in orange a brake.

This time every year, the summer visitors return. The vacationers come for a week or two; the "snowbird" retirees settle in for the duration, back from their winter sun-seeking; friends and relatives arrive for visits with us mountain-dwellers. The parking lots and trails at Mono Lake are constantly in use.

The road to Bodie State Historic Park is suddenly crowded with vehicles, with passengers experiencing a tamed version of the dusty, bumpy trip that Bodie residents endured in the last century. The steep, narrow road to Devil's Postpile National Monument and Reds Meadow opens to cars, but soon, wisely, closes to all but shuttle buses and campers' vehicles. The dirt road to Hot Creek gives folks a taste of washboards (just in case they overlooked them on the Bodie road). And Tioga Pass is open, whitening the knuckles of quite a few people who prefer their mountain highways to be flat and cliffless.

I took my son, Ryan, and his friend, Sage—a couple of 5-year old mountain men—up to Tuolumne Meadows the other day. First time this year. We'll make the trip many times during the summer. Bought our $15 Yosemite National-al Park annual pass (a bargain, especially if you use Highway 120 to travel to the Bay Area periodically). Every time we go there for a picnic it blows my mind that we live close enough to that piece of paradise for easy half-day outings.

We hiked, leisurely, along the river. The boys—all three of us—threw sticks in the water, then bombed them with rocks. We checked out the early season flowers. We picnicked. While they explored, I dozed, keeping one ear open—but they have already learned that there are hazards to avoid. As I said, they're well on their way to being mountain men. Then, on the way home, we capped the day, as always, by stopping for pie at the Tioga Pass Resort. Fantastic pie! It tastes especially good if there's an afternoon thunderstorm growling at the peaks outside.

The energy pouring so generously from the sun onto our mountains builds glorious summer thunderstorms all over the Sierra. They seldom make a significant dent in the annual precipitation counts, but what a treat for the senses—sight, smell, hearing and touch.

Summer's crisp, clear mornings warm rapidly after the sun rises. A few white puffs of cloud appear from nowhere, over the peaks. Then, by early afternoon, you suddenly realize that the clouds have thickened considerably, grown, piled up into high towers and, here and there, ominously darkened.

The clouds arrive just in time to take the edge off the heat of the day—perfect timing. A breeze kicks up. Soon you see the first lightning and are startled by the first growls of thunder. Somewhere far off you can see dark, vertical streaks where a squall has cut loose. You wish it was closer. And then you feel a drop. A big fat one. Before you can move, a shower soaks you. Or hail pummels you. Or maybe you just get teased with a few sprinkles.

It stays showery until early evening. When the sun sinks below the Sierra crest, the clouds begin to quietly, subtly, dissipate. Usually, shortly after sunset, a crystal clear mountain night reappears, packed with stars.

Two nights a week during the summer, we rangers offer star talks on the south shore of Mono Lake. Summer brings the return of many familiar friends, including the stars in the summer sky. And the Mono Basin's clear air makes it a fantastic place to lie back and lose yourself in the universe. Join us, sometime, if you would enjoy a guided tour through that night sky, punctuated with legends and stories.

Deer also return, seeking the high country after wintering in lower elevations. Unfortunately, they must cross Highway 395; the annual slaughter of road-kill deer also begins again.

At Mono Lake, 140,000 phalaropes stop over during the summer. They come from Canadian nesting areas to gorge themselves here on flies and shrimp, before leaving for autumn ranges in South America. Mono Lake is their fueling stop and rest station. California gull chicks have hatched, are growing fast, and will be up and flying by mid-July. By August, the brine shrimp numbers peak. In the summer Mono Lake is intensely alive.

Today is the summer solstice. From now, until the winter solstice, the days will grow shorter. But most of us won't notice it's happening until early September, or so, when you'll start to hear comments about how dark it is by 6 o'clock; when the summer birds have flown and the autumn migrants are arriving; when "back to school days" signs crop up in store windows, and the "snowbirds" hitch their trailers and abandon us in search of warmer winter climates.

Today we turned a corner. Welcome to summer!

# A LOVE STORY

This is a story of romance and passion, mystery and suspense, perserverance against adversity, uncertainty and heartache. But also of life's deepest satisfactions.

The couple came to the Mono Lake area in the spring of 1984. They searched for a housing site, finally locating a suitable spot to build. The imposing wooden structure took shape, eventually becoming a cozy place in which to raise a family. Both of them worked hard until they were satisfied that it was complete.

The finished structure rose high into the air, with a view of Mono Lake below, the snow-streaked eastern face of the Sierra Nevadas not far off. It was just a short trip from there to get groceries.

Everything seemed perfect, ready, anticipating the day when the first baby would appear, hopefully to be followed by others.

But that spring turned to summer, then fall, and no child was born.

They must have been disappointed. But they didn't give up. He was the "breadwinner," keeping her fed during her period of "lying in." He could be seen during those months of waiting, daily making trips toward the nearby lakes and streams, soon returning with fish for their meals.

She waited, greeting him with eager calls when he returned. Doing her part there in the family nest.

But no offspring were ever born that year. And, despite further late-season attempts at mating, the ospreys left when the fall weather turned cold, heading for somewhere warm to spend the winter.

The next spring they came back. The first pair of osprey to nest in Mono County in many, many years. They returned to the old bulky mass of sticks which they had shaped into a nest the year before. Woven around and onto the top of a large tufa tower, thirty feet above the surface of the lake, the nest had survived winter snow and several wind storms over 80 miles per hour. The pair of them went to work on home improvements, bringing branch after branch in. He did most of the carrying, while she accepted the deliveries and figured out where to add each stick.

They are beautiful, impressive creatures. Almost identical in appearance, both ospreys have wingspreads well over 5 feet, from tip to tip. Dark brown backs contrast with white undersides. But their faces are most striking: white, with a thick black streak running through the cheeks and eyes. That streak suggests a burglar's mask, or no, more like the mask of a superhero, radiating a mysterious power, slightly scary, yet admirable too.

If you could ever get close to one of them there might be plenty of reason to feel fear. Long, sharply hooked beaks look intimidating. The talons on their feet are impressively designed to impale flesh.

That second season, while the female sat in the nest, we watched from shore, a comforting half-mile buffer away from the solitude-requiring osprey. We wondered if she had actually laid any eggs, or was just sitting each day, waiting for eggs to appear. Was the lack of success last year a fluke? Maybe they were young birds, making their first attempt at parenthood. Maybe it just took some time. Who could say?

We watched the male on his trips for food. Once, while I was conducting a guided walk at the South Tufa Area, talking to a group of 25 visitors about the osprey nest offshore, at that very moment the male flew low over our heads, carrying a large fish in his talons. Those tourists were convinced that we rangers had somehow trained him to appear on cue. But this is no show at a wild animal park.

This is real life. And, sadly, that nesting season also produced no chicks.

Nor any chicks in 1986 either, their third year at Mono Lake. And none in 1987. Or 1988.

That year, after the ospreys had left the Basin in the fall, two of us took a boat out to the tufa to see if we could get a look into the nest. We were curious to know if egg shell fragments might be visible, to give us some idea whether any eggs were being laid. If fragments were there, we intended to collect some for chemical analysis. Excessively thin egg shells, due to pesticides, had been the primary reason behind a drastic decline in osprey numbers since the 1960's. But the species is also making a comeback now, since DDT has been banned in this country.

It was difficult to get a good look into the nest. The tower was too tall, too vertical, and too fragile too climb. Our boat was too small and unstable to support a ladder. We extended a camera on a long pole and took several random pictures into the nest, triggering the camera with a remote control.

If there were any pieces of egg shell, they were too tiny to show in the photographs.

I couldn't help wondering how the pair of them might have felt at the start of that sixth attempt, in 1989. Are ospreys capable of remember earlier efforts? Were they getting frustrated? Was she wondering which of them was to blame: *Is it him or me? Maybe I ought to find some other guy and...no, what am I thinking?*

We'll never know their thoughts. To us, watching from shore, the male's response each year seemed to be that if he only worked harder, kept those fish coming, brought bigger and bigger sticks for the ever-growing nest—surely no female could ask for a better mate. Surely this time...

I recall watching him lugging a stick that looked twice his length, and heavy, toward the nest from the south shore. He flew low over the water. It really looked like the branch was going to be too much for him to carry all that distance. But he approached the nest, made a mighty effort and rose up to the top of the tufa tower. Through a spotting scope I watched her take the stick from him and fiddle it into place. And moments later I watched their brief mating.

It didn't seem fair. Year after year, working so hard, making the effort, but without success.

Until the summer of 1989. One day two little heads were visible in the nest with the adults. At last! Two chicks successfully hatched. And growing bigger daily. They survivied the heat and windstorms of summer. They feasted on fish. Mornings and evenings were the best times to spot them. In the hot afternoons the chicks sheltered beneath their parents. The nest was so deep that often nothing would show at those times.

The growing chicks got fairly active as time went on. I worried they might fall out. Maybe that's why the nests are built so massive and deep—to serve as safe playpens, besides their other purposes of shelter and warmth.

We worried, and still do, about human disturbance. Occasionally people in canoes would go past the warning buoys we'd placed in a perimeter around the nest tufa. The parents would be noticeably upset. Too much of that kind of hassle and they might leave this area.

Should we keep their presence here a secret then? Or post signs on shore along with the buoys on the lake? Go for the educational approach, relying on the fact that not many people boat here and most of them would gladly comply with our requests?

Well, you're reading this. That should be a clue how we decided to handle things. I learned a long time ago that it is almost impossible to protect something that very few people know about. With knowledge comes understanding and caring.

Most of you will have to watch the ospreys from the south shore of Mono Lake. Oh, yes, they are still here. The count to date is 2 chicks in 1989, 1 in '90, and 2 in '91. Through standard-power binoculars you can just barely make out the white and black contrast of their faces. You can see them eating—but the distance is too great to tell what kind of fish they've caught. And, if they are again successful this summer, you may be able to watch young birds on the edge of the nest, practicing with their growing wings, beating the air each day. Until that special moment arrives when they leave the nest for a first short flight to a nearby tufa tower.

Ospreys, the fish-eating hawks, raising their babies right here at Mono Lake, the fishless inland sea. It's a story of romance and passion, mystery and suspense, perserverance against adversity, uncertainty and heartache. But also of life's deepest satisfactions.

# THE PHALAROPE

A woman walked along the sandy shore of Mono Lake. It was summer. A ground squirrel stood up straight, staring at her as she approached, then scurried into the nearby grass and disappeared into its burrow. Alkali flies massed on the beach, but whisked away from her feet as she ambled along.

Her attention was focused on the water of the lake. Hundreds of birds were scattered across the surface. She recognized most of them as sea gulls, but there were smaller birds too. She watched several of the delicate-looking shorebirds pecking at the water, wondering why many of them spun in tight circles periodically.

She was not watching where her feet were going. That's how she stubbed her toe on the bottle.

It hurt. Her big toe, exposed in her sandal, throbbed painfully. Why was she so clumsy? Things like that were always happening to her. She bent to pick up the bottle, prepared to hurl it far away, but stopped.

It was not a belated sense of guilt at tossing someone's trash into the lake that stopped her. It was the weight and appearance of the bottle. It had an alien air; some sort of dark glass flask, with curious patterns decorating its sides.

She twisted at the cork which stoppered the bottle. When it finally worked loose, a genie appeared in a must-smelling cloud of vapor.

"Thank you, mistress, for releasing me. As a reward, I grant you the standard three wishes."

As you might imagine, she stammered the standard exclamations of surprise and disbelief, before she stopped wasting time and considered her wishes.

"If I can really change my life...have the things I've always wanted...this is so hard!" She kicked at the sand, which made her hurt toe throb. "I wish I was graceful, and beautiful. No! Not exactly that. I wish...I wish I could fly. Soar through the sky like a swift, graceful bird."

The genie looked sourly at her. "I don't think you understand how this works. If I was a stickler for accuracy you would've already used up your three wishes. But I think I perceive the essence of your desire. That's number one. Be more careful about the next two."

Her next two wishes were much clearer. "I've always wanted to travel; to see distant lands. Please? And for number three, I wish my husband would take more of a hand with the kids." She rushed to explain. "I mean, if I'm going to travel, someone's got to stay home and take care of things. He's just always left the children to me—at least the real work that goes with raising kids. So if you're going to grant wish number two and let me travel, you'd better take care of my husband and the kids while you're at it."

She sighed, satisfied, but wondering if she ought to have asked for gold and jewels instead. Oh well, it was done.

And it was. The genie did his thing, and her wishes were granted.

******

A group of twenty people were walking along the sandy shore of Mono Lake. Their leader wore the Smokey the Bear hat of a park ranger. He stopped and pointed toward a flock of small birds on the lake.

"Those are Wilson's phalaropes. See the buffy color on their necks and the black streak on the head? They've just recently arrived here from Canada, where they nest. They only weigh about one ounce when they reach the lake after that long flight. But they get busy, fattening on flies and shrimp, and within 30 days have doubled their body weight.

"Think about that! Thank about what *you* weigh, right now. Consider what you'd have to do to double that in just one month. The phalaropes find so much food here that they can get very fat, very fast. They use the fat to fuel their migration south, when they leave. After a couple months here they will fly down to South America for the winter. And they won't even stop to feed on the way. They'll fly 2000 miles in just two days, non-stop. Mono Lake is their essential 'gas station' and 'rest area.'"

The group watched the flock of birds. They looked so tiny and frail, it was hard to accept that they were such world travelers, moving between northern Canada and South America, then back again, every spring and fall.

"140,000 phalaropes visit Mono Lake each summer. We see these Wilson's phalaropes first, then red-necked phalaropes later in the summer. The...oh, look!"

Something caused the entire flock of birds to take to the air. Several hundred phalaropes, wings rapidly beating, climbed up, then made the crowd gasp as they began to move like a single organism. Dark backs suddenly disappeared, replaced by white breasts as each bird turned. Since all of the phalaropes turned in unison, the effect was stunning. It was something like a school of tropical fish moving as one body in an aquarium. For a few moments, the flock put on a precision drill-team show, flashing back and forth over the lake, spiralling high, before settling back onto the water, right where they had begun.

Then, one of the phalaropes swam boldly toward the people standing at the shore, pecking at flies on the water-surface as it approached. It paused after each peck and stared at the ranger, as though it were listening to him and understood his words.

"All of these phalaropes are females. I find it fascinating that, in the nesting areas up north, after each female lays her eggs, she leaves. Comes down here to Mono Lake. Meanwhile, the male is left to sit on the eggs, hatch the chicks and care for them until they can fly. *Then* the males and young birds migrate. It's an interesting reversal of sex roles."

The crowd laughed when a young woman raised a fist and said "right on!" Several couples with kids in tow exchanged male-female looks."

The phalarope had continued to inch closer and closer to shore. When the crowd laughed, the phalarope began spinning.

"Look. Is she celebrating her women's liberation?" someone asked the ranger.

"Could be. More likely, she's just hungry. Phalaropes will spin in tight circles like that to stir up food and concentrate it into a little whirlpool. See how she's stopped and begun eating now? "She's a beauty, isn't she? So tiny and graceful. I'm really glad that Mono Lake is here for these birds. It's important to recognize that, should this lake's ecosystem die, places in South America and Canada might be affected." He turned, prepared to lead the group farther down the shore, when his foot kicked a bottle half-buried in the sand.

The ranger picked up the bottle. He examined it curiously for a moment, tipping it over. A little sand spilled out. He shrugged and, as he continued walking, put the bottle into his daypack with other bits of litter he had gathered since the start of the tour.

# TAKE A TOUR

When they say, "Ooh!"—with the exclamation point, I know things are going well.

A visit to Mono Lake can generate a lot of "oohs" and "ahs." This place is so different, offers such startling and unusual scenery and sights. Some of the discoveries are immediate and obvious—like the tufa towers on the south shore, with their variety of shapes and textures. Or the amazing contrast of miles of blue water surrounded by desert shrubs, with the snowy Sierra crest as a backdrop.

But some of the discoveries are more subtle. I know, from talking to thousands of visitors, that fascinating details can be missed during a casual, quick stop. We put up exhibit panels and provide brochures to try to fill in the gaps. And every summer day, rangers and naturalists conduct guided walks.

We call this part of our job "interpretation." Our kind of intepreter translates the information about the area into a language that visitors can understand. If you only come to Mono Lake once in your life, it would be a shame to miss some of the easy, important discoveries. If you are lucky enough to be able to explore this area frequently, our staff members hope to give you helpful background information for your own self-discoveries.

Would you like to go on a tour? Here are some of the things you might do and see:

A Forest Service or State Reserve naturalist will greet you at the South Tufa Area parking lot. That is the main visitor site at Mono Lake; it is part of the Mono Basin National Forest Scenic Area. Both agencies share the schedule of tours.

You'll walk down a trail toward the center of the tufa grove. What's a tufa and why does Mono Lake have them? You'll have to learn about the lake's unique water chemistry to understand the tufa towers. You may find yourself participating in making some tufa, on the spot, by mixing lake water—with its high carbonate content—into freshwater—containing calcium, like the springs which enter the lake. The end product is calcium carbonate—tufa—a solid produced by the mixing of waters.

In fact, you'll find that everything at Mono Lake is influenced by the salty, alkaline character of the water. Rub some of it between your fingers. It will feel like soapy dishwater. That's the carbonates, the dissolved baking soda. It makes the water harsh, helps form tufa towers, and makes it impossible for fish to live here.

But you won't have trouble locating the life which *has* adapted to the lake's harsh conditions. Alkali flies crowd the shore this time of year. Don't worry, the alkali flies are shy. They don't like people and they won't bother you. Look under water, near shore, and you'll see them walking, enclosed in air bubbles.

The ranger will show you the fly larva and pupa stages on the submerged rocks. Birds eat the adult flies and the larvae. The Paiute Indians used to harvest the abundant pupae too. Would you like to taste one? It's a new experience you may not want to miss. This was a staple of the local Indians' diet, and a valuable item for trade to other Indians.

Have you heard something about the water problems of Mono Lake? Who hasn't, by now?

As you start to look at the life in the water, realize that much of the controversy surrounds the likelihood that the lake's creatures will not be able to adapt to greater salinity levels as the lake shrinks. The flies are already showing the effects, and researchers can predict the levels where the falling lake will no longer provide suitable habitat for their survival.

Brine shrimp—the other animal found in large numbers—are also at risk. You can easily catch them in containers provided by the tour guide. The lake teems with the half-inch long shrimp in the summer, adding up to millions of pounds of the tiny creatures. They are a species unique to Mono Lake, a species which has adapted to the unique conditions of this ancient chemical soup.

As long as the flies and shrimp are able to survive they will be important food for over a million birds that visit the lake each year. California gulls come here to eat the "shrimp soup" and nest on islands in the lake. Even more birds migrate here from nesting grounds in Canada. This lake is their rest-stop and "gas station" on long migrations between Canada and Central and South America.

Which birds will you see on your tour? The gulls are almost always easy to find; you can watch them feeding. The young born this year are easy to tell because of their brown color, though they look as big as the adults.

Thousands of phalaropes are here mid-summer, but the lake is big and it's a matter of luck whether they'll be hanging around the south shore on any given day. The eared grebes start to arrive in late August.

Watch for killdeer, violet-green swallows, Brewer's blackbirds, sandpipers—any of over 90 bird species found around the lake.

Volcanoes will be mentioned during your tour. Mono Lake is ringed on three sides by volcanoes, has volcanic islands, and you'll be walking on volcanic pumice and obsidian chips along its shore. If the lake's chemistry is the controlling factor for so much found here, volcanoes are one of the primary factors behind that particular blend of chemicals.

There is a lot of variety on the tours. Some of my favorite moments have been totally unpredictable. Several times an osprey, a fish-eating hawk that nests on a tufa tower, has flown right over my group holding a fish in its talons. Fish at Mono Lake? No, but it is only a few air miles over to Rush Creek and Grant Lake Reservoir.

One day, a weasel put on a wild show for us. Occasionally we'll see one of the sleek little hunters streaking past, running from tufa-shelter to tufa-shelter. But for some reason, this day, the weasel kept popping back out, racing again and again between one tufa and another, and now and then pausing to look at us, as if to make sure we were admiring his performance.

Mono Lake is a very special place. Understanding and appreciation of those qualities is the overriding objective of our tours. We have some other sub-themes. Destroying the false image of a "dead sea" is easy, once people learn about the super-abundance of life the lake supports.

We hope people will incorporate what they discover here into their own personal conclusions about the water-issue questions. If nothing else, after visiting the lake they should have a clearer idea of what's at stake. We don't proselytize a position on the water issue—legislation which created the Reserve and Scenic Area keeps the agencies from that role—but we try hard to educate people about the facts and the positions taken by both sides. We trust that Mono Lake sells itself as a place to care about.

Join us for a tour. Don't be surprised if you find yourself "ooh-ing" and "ah-ing" as you explore the mysteries of tufa towers, catch a few brine shrimp, float bits of pumice rock in the lake, and maybe even take a fly-pupae snack break along the way.

# TSK TSK TAMARISK

The pruning shears slip off the taproot; this one is too thick. I'll have to cut all ten of the stems which rise from the root ball one by one. Grunting, I wipe the sweat from my eyes and mentally curse, again, that unknown genius who first introduced tamarisk to the North American deserts. Little did he know what he was starting. I suspect he thought he was doing something worthwhile; bringing a plant from the Middle East which would grow well in dry, salty environments; creating shade-thickets where only scrub growth had been.

Yet the years have gone by and those first tamarisk plants have become "The Tamarisk Problem." So I cut...and sweat...and mentally curse.

Tamarisk, also called saltcedar, is a non-native—which makes it a target for eradication in national and state parks and other places where native ecosystems are supposed to be protected. Reason enough for us to go after it in the Mono Lake Tufa State Reserve.

But there are lots of other non-natives we don't mess with. Mostly because the European annual grasses and Russian thistles (the ubiquitous tumbleweeds) and suchlike, are so widespread that any efforts would be futile. If we, somehow, once removed all such plants from within our boundaries, they would soon be re-invading once again.

Tamarisk gets targeted because it is not so prevalent and, most of all, because of its incredible thirst. As a shrub or tree, in dense thickets, it can suck a source of surface water dry. It's insatiable. Better at drinking up groundwater than the willows which it associates with—until it completely chokes them out. At Mono Lake we are particularly sensitive to losses of water. So we fight on.

I wish I could confront the culprit who brought them in, just once. Or was it done unknowingly, by seeds that hitched a ride half-way around the world until they found a place to set down roots?

Thinking these thoughts as I uproot another plant, I suddenly see a connection with a question a Mono Lake visitor asked me earlier in the day. "How could they have ever allowed the water diversions from Mono Lake's streams in the first place? Didn't anyone see what was bound to happen here?"

It's a common enough reaction, based on 20-20 hindsight, heard most often from visitors from other countries or states—it's easier to sit back and criticize when distance insures that you don't have a personal stake in the history or issues.

The answer is that over fifty years ago a *few* people did point out changes which would occur when this salty lake was forced to shrink. Anyone who gave it some thought knew that the lake's salts would gradually be concentrated. Whether or not the living ecosystem could handle the change was a more uncertain question. I suspect most people figured that was an issue that they could comfortably put off considering for, oh, at least fifty years or so; perhaps until the distant 1980s.

And who worries about things so far off in the future?

Do we *really* think much about what will be going on in the summer of 2041? Sure, we say we want our children and grandchildren to have a good life. But how real does it seem? If there are problems of some sort, issues that come up in our community that might have long-term consequences, are we able to predict those things accurately and then relate realistically to those predictions?

You know the kinds of things I'm thinking about. Consider, just to pick one, the hole in the ozone layer. People started messing up the atmosphere a long, long time ago. It accelerated in the last fifty years, I'm sure. But, according to what I read, the culprit is *us*, and despite some measures our government has taken already, those of us who run refrigerators and air conditioners (does he mean me?) are daily contributing to the problem.

Slather on the sunscreen, hope you aren't in the statistical percentage that will get deadly skin cancer, and go on doing what you gotta do each day. What else can we do?

It's one of those distant, long-term problems. The payoff is way down the line. Right? Maybe they'll come up with a cure, a solution, some magic technological—or if it comes to that, medical—fix. Whoever "they" are.

Fifty years from now I'm going to be 90 years old. (And still going strong, needless to say). I hope that my planet is healthy. I hope that the human population of the world will have stopped its wild growth. I don't like to think about what it will be like for my children, or geriatric old me, if the developers develop all the natural beauty out of the world. I hope that "they" figure out some way to decontaminate all the radioactive waste we have already generated, let alone that which might be produced by nuclear reactors between now and then—because I *truly* cannot relate to safely storing something so toxic for hundreds of thousands of years, let alone fifty.

Gosh, there's plenty to worry about. It isn't much fun to dwell on it. I strongly suspect that the reason the Mono Lake stream diversions sailed past decision-making bodies in the 1930s is that the problems seemed far-off, not certain, and the benefit—water to Los Angeles—was so immediate.

I strongly suspect that whoever brought tamarisk to the western deserts had no idea a park ranger would someday be sweating, cutting and mentally cursing that person's typical—very human—lack of forethought.

So, if history shows that we aren't very good at forecasting into the distant future, what's the lesson here?

How about "Do your best"? Let's be careful with our environment; err on the side of conservative stewardship. Try—knowing we'll most likely fail—to think beyond the present and gratification of our own immediate interests.

It's starting to look like our society, through citizen involvement and the courts, will step in and save Mono Lake from a slow death set in motion—by society—over 50 years ago. That's great. Meanwhile, on the local front, I'll go on clearing out this grove of pesky tamarisk.

# A SUMMER GATHERING AND A
# WOMAN SCORNED

 You have to pity those poor, deprived urbanites. In the mountains we've got all the bright lights nighttime action they seldom get back home. What I always wonder is how you're goin' to keep 'em down in the city once they've seen a mountain summer night.

Of course they've got plenty of those incandescent and neon types of lights—lots more than we do. But that's a big part of their problem. With all that artificial glow cluttering up the atmosphere, not to mention the toxic gunk that also obscures urban night skies, they've gone and spoiled the free nightly show.

Memorial Day weekend, 1991, marked the start of an exceptional gathering of stars and heavenly bodies which occured every night that summer. Admission was free. You could pull up a chair, or a blanket, or just lay back, resting your head on something comfortable (soft grass, a beach blanket, a friendly friend's shoulder). The show began at dusk and ended when you couldn't keep your eyes open any longer.

No, I'm not talking about the Sierra Summer Festival. Our clear mountain skies mean we have excellent front-row seats for stargazing. But the Summer of '91 was exceptional.

Most of the stars and constellations ("pictures" made by groups of stars) are regulars in the cast. You probably already know the Big Dipper. It is almost straight overhead mid-summer. Starting from that familiar shape, using a star chart, you can locate the most obvious constellations in the sky: the Little Dipper—which includes the north star; Cassiopeia—like a big "W" toward the northern horizon; Leo, the Lion, whose head and mane look a lot like a sickle off the Russian flag—now in the west; and Böotes the herdsman, which resembles a big kite or ice cream cone off the handle-end of the big dipper.

But the exceptional summer gathering that year was by planets. Venus, Jupiter and Mars put on a spectacular show, low in the west, for several hours after sunset. Unless the mountain crest was blocking your view, you couldn't miss Venus. It's the third brightest thing we ever see in the sky. (Can you name the first and second?) On Memorial Day, looking west, Jupiter was the bright light above and to the left of Venus. With a small telescope or spotting scope you could see several of Jupiter's moons. Reddish Mars was lurking between the two bright planets, not so spectacular. Nothing like two summers before when it was closer to Earth in its orbit and shone brightly enough to stand out from the distant stars.

These three planets came within a 20 degree arc of each other in May. But planets are travelers. By mid-June, as they shifted around in their individual orbits, they appeared to be almost on top of each other—within 3 degrees.

To add to the beauty of the planets' gathering, several bright stars were also nearby. We could see the Gemini twins, Pollux and Castor, just above Venus and to the right of Mars. The Greeks gave us the twins legend, but I also like the Australian aborigine story about this pair. The two stars are hunters, chasing a kangaroo (another bright star,

Capella, farther north). Every year when the two disappear to the north it marks the beginning of a great hot season—because the hunters finally catch the kangaroo and are roasting it.

There was another good celestial show at the opposite end of the stage that holiday weekend—the full moon. As always, the full moon rose just at sunset. Its bright light made it harder to see some dim stars, but the primary star and planet display was way over to the west anyway and not affected much.

Do you know why the moon changes shape? It's not always full, of course. Every month it goes through the entire range, declining from full to crescent to nothing and then, happily, growing back again. Some explain this changeable nature with talk of angles to the sun as the moon goes around the earth in its monthly orbit. But I prefer this Paiute legend, out of Utah (adapted from *Why The North Star Stands Still* by William R. Palmer, Prentice-Hall):

The Moon is actually the wife of the Sun Man. The lonely Sun Man, who must be at his job every day, moving the Sun across the sky, was much more happy in his work after a village maiden agreed to be his wife and join him in the heavens. To make her beautiful in the Sun Man's eyes, Shinob, the Great Spirit, turned her shiny and golden and made her round, like the ball of the sun. But trouble came when she paid her first visit back to her home village. Stopping to see her reflection in a lake, she became ecstatic about her glowing appearance, and bounced along with joy until she reached the village. The unsuspecting villagers suddenly saw a giant, yellow ball bouncing into town. Instead of greeting her with joy, praising her great beauty, they ran in terror! She was furious at this reception, and began bouncing onto houses, flattening them, causing great destruction, and even bouncing onto people and killing them! Well! To punish her and protect the villagers from future attacks like this, some of her golden light was taken away and she was banished to the night sky, away from her loving husband. Furthermore, to keep her from being able to bounce, Shinob took some of her roundness away every day. But he made sure she always grew back because she was now The Moon, giver of light at night and marker of the passage of time: there are twelve "moons," or months in each year.

Isn't that a great explanation? But the part I like best is that, since the Sun Man and Moon are still husband and wife, every so often they are allowed to come together for a love-meeting in the sky. Some privacy is called for here, so the lights are turned away from Earth for awhile. Scientists, with little romance in their hearts, now call these meetings "eclipses."

Summer brings "bright lights action" every night in the mountains, but that Memorial Day weekend a gathering of celestial bodies and the "woman scorned" in all her glory put on a special show for the Mono Basin.

Autumn

# FALLING!

 **D**eath or glory? An ending or a promise? I know a few people who hate this season. But autumn is my favorite time of the year.

It happened the Sunday before last. Did you notice? It is no longer summer. September 23 was the autumnal equinox—the first official day of the fall season. The weather did not tell the story. In fact, to judge by the weather autumn began in late August this year, when it got downright cold. But we then returned to baking hot summer weather in early September. The change to true autumn weather comes gradually, in fits and starts.

What tends to escape our notice is the equinox itself. Ever since spring there have been more daylight hours than darkness. It goes back to the fact that our globe is on a tilted axis. As we travel once around the sun each year, our northern half of the globe is tilted more directly toward the sun during the summer and more away from it in the winter. That produces the changes in day length and gives us two transition days called "equinoxes," when daylight and nighttime are equal length.

But it is the "fall" aspects of fall which seem to get some people down. Leaves fall off trees. Daylight surrenders to long dark nights. Campgrounds close; Tioga and Sonora Passes eventually close, businesses close down in Mammoth during the autumn doldrums. All that depressing stuff.

Turn it around, I say. Take a closer look.

Fall is a treat for the senses. We get fantastic fall color in this part of the world. One of my favorite aspen groves is up Lundy Canyon, where you can drive into a golden tunnel of overhead branches, park by the creek and wander among the trees. Marvel at the effect of sunlight passing through the yellow leaves, then turn around and see what it does when reflected off a solid, shimmering wall of color. Even the shrublands produce color in early fall. Rabbitbrush blooms and willow leaves turn shades of canary, lemon and orange. We don't get a lot of New England-style hues, but check those impenetrable wild rose thickets on the hillsides—burgundy red.

Still, all those pretty leaves are dying. It's the loss of green chlorophyll as they die which allows us to see the other colors. That's not sad; no more than the loss of dead skin cells and fingernails that is always going on with our own bodies. Most of the trees and shrubs we admire so much are perennials, just shutting down to protect themselves from winter cold. Not death, but a part of their ongoing, long-term approach to life.

There are a lot of annual plants which do die, of course. But their off-spring will be back, come spring. In fact, many of the seeds *need* the conditions of winter to successfully reproduce. Winter snows will freeze, heave and turn the soil, preparing it for growth as a farmer might with his plow. Winter storms and snowmelt will scour drainages and abrade tough seed coats, permitting the seeds to sprout.

The same goes for some animals which die in the fall. Mono Lake brine shrimp will die by the trillions when the lake gets cold. But all summer they produced eggs which sank into the mud under the lake. Those egg-cysts *must* go through enough days at low temperatures and low oxygen levels—winter conditions—if they are to hatch successfully. The cooling of autumn and winter also causes Mono Lake and every other deep lake around here to "turn over." In the summer the upper surfaces are warmer. When it cools, that upper layer sinks and mixes with the deeper water. Nutrients which had sunk to the bottom are stirred up. Those nutrients fertilize the aquatic plants which support the rest of the lake's food chain. The life we see in the lakes in the spring and summer depends on this cold season.

Fall does bring a change of pace. It is a time of slowing down and settling quiet. Sure, most tourists are gone. I know there would be economic benefits if the area was truly a year-round resort. But isn't it nice that we do have some off times? By Labor Day, every year, I am really looking forward to the relative quiet of September. But October is even better. The autumn colors are here, but the weather is unsettled enough to scare off even more tourists. We've got the beauty and peace of the Eastern Sierra autumn to ourselves. You can't make much money running a business, I realize. But what the heck, close up shop and take a walk. Enjoy.

There's the joy of breathing fall air—crisp, clean, you can make a meal of breathing. There's the mystery of the migrating flocks of birds, particularly in the numbers seen at Mono Lake. How nice it is to see a roly poly squirrel or, if you're lucky, a bear—stuffed and fat—cramming just a bit more food into itself before settling down to a winter sleep. Something's sensuous and harvest-happy about that.

Autumn is my favorite season because it is a transition. Summer and winter, around here, seem to arrive and stay. Autumn and spring are fleeting. As such, they are promises. The longer I live here and absorb the seasonal patterns, the more I can see that autumn is one part of a beautiful whole.

When do I like autumn least? When I'm stuck indoors. You have to brave the blustery weather of this season to appreciate its offerings. Returning back to your warm house, a fireplace, a cup of hot cider, feasts, friends and family—these are other delicious parts of the seasonal pattern.

Fall is contrast: hot and cold, activity and slumber, constantly changing weather, colors and stark contrasts, death and glory, an ending...a promise.

# THE MYSTERY OF THE RED-EYED BIRD

 **T**hey come in the gloom of the night when no human eyes are watching. Silently, dark shapes with red eyes descend from the sky. Thousands upon thousands blanket the black surface of the lake. They keep on coming. Alfred Hitchcock never dared dream of a bird invasion of such scale. Soon three-quarters of a million avian invaders are here. We call them eared grebes because of a pair of feather crests which decorate their heads in breeding season.

An autumn dawn at Mono Lake allows human visitors their first look at the nighttime arrivals. At first all you may notice are lots of dark dots out on the water. Look through binoculars and you will see that they are small, duck-like birds. Then begin to focus across mile after mile of the surface of this big lake. From the south shore it is nine miles across. You may see eared grebes crowding the water through that entire distance.

800,000 eared grebes come to Mono Lake in the fall. That is one heck of a lot of birds of just one type. We do not really know how many eared grebes there are in the world.

Some guess that one-quarter of the entire species is here on this lake, all at once.

They come from nesting grounds in Canada. They will stay at Mono Lake until the food supply disappears, as brine shrimp die off in the cold weather of November or December. Then the grebes head for Central America to overwinter. At least we know they end up down there. No one ever witnesses their night-time arrival and departures.

Grebes seem mysterious in other ways. Their looks are rather strange. They have a dark back, whitish underparts (which you can see best along the throat), a small light cheek-patch, and those unusual red eyes.

They spend a good part of their life under water. Eared grebes have lobed toes to help them swim. Not webbed, like ducks, but more as if you had a fringe of tissue sticking out from either side of your fingers. But the real strange aspect of the body design is the location of their legs.

Think of a penguin. Its legs are at one end of its body, so it stands upright on land, much like a human. Underwater, those legs become propellers, located at the back end of the bird, perfectly placed to shove them along most efficiently. Eared grebes have "propeller legs" at their rear ends too, but they are not designed like penguin's. They swim great underwater, but cannot stand up on land.

If you ever see an eared grebe on solid ground, something is wrong. Every so often someone finds one and brings it to us. Who knows why or how they came to be on land, but once there, they became helpless to take off again. Did I mention that eared grebes seem to be weak fliers? At least they have to work hard to take off from the water. They cannot get moving at all from land—not even stand upright. The concerned people think the bird must be sick, since it sits so quietly. Every time this has happened we have taken the grebe to the lake and, happily, it has sped off across the water, until it was out far enough to dive.

They can stay underwater for a long time. It is a way to escape, but is used more when they are hungry. The grebes dive for brine shrimp at Mono Lake. They seem to spend almost as much time underwater as on top of it. If you have ever gone swimming in the harsh alkaline water of this lake, you may remember how it can sting your eyes. Come to think of it, maybe that's why the grebes have red eyes. You'd have red eyes too if you dove under Mono Lake all day with your eyes open.

Actually, there is a theory that the red color helps the grebes see better in the underwater gloom. It has something to do with wavelengths and penetrability through the water. Think of amber foglights on a car—same general idea.

The most impressive thing of all, the thing everyone keeps coming back to when they talk about these birds, is their number. Along with the other fall migrants and the birds that have been here all summer, the grebes help make autumn the "birdiest" time of year at Mono Lake.

Sometimes they mass so closely together that it seems like you could walk across the lake on the backs of grebes. Think about that number—800,000—for a moment. If each grebe takes up about 12 inches, and they sat end to end, they would extend 150 miles! Good thing Mono Lake has about 60 square miles of surface where they can spread out.

Their combined weight totals somewhere in the vicinity of 100,000 pounds. Who cares, you ask? The amazing thing about their weight is that they will double it here in just 30 days, gorging themselves on brine shrimp. That's a clue as to just how many shrimp the lake produces (millions of pounds of the tiny little creatures!).

The irony of all this is that Mono Lake is still referred to by some misinformed writers as a "dead sea." In truth, it is a super-productive ecosystem, supporting far more life than the fresh-water lakes of this area—relative deserts by comparison.

I am impressed by eared grebes. They help to make Mono Lake unique. They remind us of the importance of this place to other sites thousands of miles away in Canada and Central America.

But I have to admit that I don't relate well to them. They fly by night. They spend a lot of time underwater where I can't see what they are up to. They are almost always silent. They hang around in enormous crowds that only a New Yorker could love.

Some mysterious night, late in the fall, they will startle us again by disappearing into the gloom. Soon after, somewhere in Central America, dark, silent, red-eyed figures will descend from the sky.

# NOSES, ROSES AND ROOTS

This should be interesting. Could be strange. I've popped my pills and inhaled stuff up my nose. Had two injections just the other day. Yet I still feel fragile, as though the stuff will overwhelm me if I'm not careful. I think I'll go shut the windows and doors.

You're not thinking what I think you're thinking are you? You've been watching too many TV cop shows. The pills are antihistimines and and the inhalant is prescribed by my allergist. And without the monthly shots I might have to leave Mono County in the late summer and early Fall.

It's hay fever season. Park rangers shouldn't be afflicted this way, seems to me. I'm a friend to all nature, after all. Yet the beautiful, yellow blossoms of rabbitbrush and the inconspicuous greenish flowers of sagebrush leer at me, threatening me with their heavy loads of pollen. "Just one little breeze," they seem to say, "and you can eat our dust. We'll show you arrogant people what lifeforms are *really* dominant around here."

Excuse me while I sneeze.

This was a great year for the shrubs, for some reason. Back in late Spring and early Summer the pink desert peach blossoms and yellow bitterbrush put on the best show I've seen in ten years. Maybe it was because of the quantity and timing of our March storms. I kind of hoped that whatever conditions produced such heavy Spring flowering of shrubs would no longer be at work this late in the year. Futile hope.

Got to open another box of Kleenex.

Actually, the allergist's shots have helped a lot. I no longer feel like I'm going to drown when I lay down to sleep at night.

Sagebrush is subtle stuff. Ubiquitous, yet subtle. Everyone notices the golden rabbitbrush blossoms; can't miss them. But sagebrush is sly. Its flower stalks are the same color as the rest of the plant—grayish green. Until they start dumping out pollen. Even then the stalks just assume a tarnished, greenish-gold appearance. A lot of local hayfever sufferers blame their problems on the rabbitbrush. But the sneaky sage is just as busy invading our nasal passages with pollen.

Did you know that the state flower of Nevada is sagebrush? Interesting people in that state.

My lucky wife is not susceptible to hayfever, even though we share a job which requires both of us to wade through the pollen ocean each day. We used to work in state parks on the other side of the mountains, where poison oak is ubiquitous. Poison oak never bothered me much. But Janet's so susceptible that I've probably given her a case just now by typing those two words: poison oak. I use to come home from work and strip, throw all my work clothes into a special bag she never touched, take a shower, and *then* give her a kiss. We developed this system after our marriage was endangered one too many times by poison oak rashes she developed in intimate spots traced back to you know who.

There's always something, I guess. Poison oak, for some. Sagebrush allergies for others. Floods, fires, earthquakes, hurricanes—few places are without their natural challenges to humans. If we choose to live here for the benefits this area offers most of the time, we have to put up with the seasonal challenges. And the episodic challenges too. Someday the volcanoes around here will erupt again. It's inevitable; part of the natural environment between Mono Lake and Mammoth.

"The problem is the Rose Parade."

I was talking to an elderly man at Mono Lake. We had been discussing California's many environmental problems, agreeing that the ultimate root issue was population. After I commented that as of April 1, 1991 there were over 30 million people in this state, he blamed the Rose Parade.

You may be as bewildered as I was, wondering how he was going to tie the two things together.

"That's the only day in the entire year," he said, "when the weather is nice in Southern California. Never fails. Every other day Pasadena has horrible smog. All those folks watching the parade on TV back in Minnesota, or wherever, compare the blizzard out their windows to those darn sunny New Year's days on TV, and right away start packing to move out here."

Eureka! One of those fundamental truths. The Rose Parade, with its deceitful weather, is behind immigration into Southern California. Humans migrating in search of greener pastures.

I suppose I could migrate to somewhere without sagebrush and rabbitbrush. Find some state park where I wouldn't have to work right in among the stuff; where no volcanoes threaten my neighborhood.

But I have learned the lesson of the Rose Parade. And I know that, with 30 million Californians crowding this state, I prefer to live in good old sparsely populated Mono County. Where only one town has any traffic lights. Where I don't have to lock my doors at night. Where the deer and the antelope play.

I've learned to look on the bright side. After all, a good hay fever season shows that the plants are healthy, busily celebrating being alive. In the face of drought, windstorms, alkaline soils and freezing winters, sagebrush and rabbitbrush dig in and thrive.

I've put down roots here too. No runny nose is going to run me off.

But maybe I'll buy stock in Kleenex.

# DROUGHT DREAMS

"*Californians should realize that a five-year drought is normal...tree rings, core samples from glaciers...show droughts that have lasted 20 years over the last several hundred years.*" *Sunset Magazine, November, 1991*

I know, I know. That's the last thing any of us wanted to read just now. But outside my window it is warm and clear. That wonderful early snow storm in October which was "supposed" to be the first of a whole series, begins to look like a real teaser. Five prior years of drought have made this pattern look awfully familiar: high pressure over California blocks the Pacific storms; the Rockies and mid-west get dumped on while our state suffers unwanted warmth and clear skies.

And, as a result, various people around these parts dream troubled dreams. Drought dreams. What if? Ooh, don't think about it. But what if...what if the drought continues this winter? Or for two more years? Or *ten* more?

Scary. Scary for ski areas and hotels and developers and farmers and all kinds of businesses, but scary for every single one of us, too.

Here's a thought—maybe all those potential immigrants to California, seeing that there's too little water here, would change their plans. Far as I'm concerned a decline in our population would help in many ways to improve the quality of life. But it'd be a shame if extended drought was the only way for that to happen.

Things could get harsh.

Well, maybe it won't happen. Not now, anyway. Statistically, of course, 20 year droughts are almost certain to reoccur *sometime.* But, like "the big earthquake" for communities along the San Andreas fault, and "the big volcanic eruptions" around here, we can hope they will come in someone else's lifetime. Statistically that's a pretty good hope.

Since I work at Mono Lake and live near its shore, my personal drought nightmare goes something like this:

It is the year 2004. 63 years ago Mono Lake began to decline because people diverted streams away from the lake to Los Angeles; the lake dropped 44 feet by 1991. But at that time scientists and citizens, alarmed by the increase in salinity as the lake shrank, won court victories which seemed to insure that the decline would be stopped short of total collapse of the ecosystem. Trillions of brine shrimp and alkali flies would, it appeared, be able to go on living, becoming food for over a million birds. One of the most productive and unique lake ecosystems in the world was going to be preserved. Things looked so optimistic thirteen years ago.

Yet, although no stream diversions have been allowed since that time, the lake *continues* to drop anyway; about one-and-a-half feet in each of these dry years. The drought began in 1987, seventeen incredibly dry years ago. *All* the available run-off during this drought has not been enough to replace water lost from evaporation.

And because of the 44 foot decline that had already occurred, now the lake is at the point of death. It was inexorable. Unavoidable. Despite the court orders. Despite the best intentions of a concerned—now helpless— public. The natural buffer which would have protected the lake from even this exceptional drought disappeared between 1941 and 1989.

Scientists had predicted the effects we have all seen as the lake dropped, but they were assuming continued human diversion of streams, not endless dry years. The lake was at 6374 feet in 1991. Nine years later, at the turn of the century (remember the celebrations, our hopes at reaching the magical year 2000—was it only four years ago?), with the lake at 6359 feet, the alkali flies were history. Populations of all other species were declining.

But the brine shrimp, the real key to the lake's productivity—a unique species found no where in the world except Mono Lake—hung on a few more years. While the lake continued to plummet. Now, by this summer's end, Mono Lake will be at 6352 feet. A study published back in 1988 concluded with unfortunate accuracy that at that level comes "the demise of the present lake ecosystem." Mono Lake is in its final death throes—even though we humans stopped diverting its streams thirteen years ago, fully intending to "Save Mono Lake."

Scientists, in this horrible dream, have been scrambling to salvage samples of the algae, shrimp and flies, hoping to somehow keep some alive to "reseed" a recovered lake. Someday, maybe this *next* winter, the drought must break; the lake basin will refill, diluting the salts. But it's doubtful that scientists have the ability to keep eggs or cysts or any portion of the life cycle alive in laboratories very long. Maybe someday they will figure out how to grow a new shrimp from a genetic sample alone. It's the twenty-first century, but they aren't there yet.

Shudder. Wake up screaming and sweating. Send the script idea to Steven King.

Pray for snow.

Winter

# HAPPY QUIET

Like everyone else in the Eastern Sierra, the rangers at Mono Lake had been waiting, wondering when it would ever turn to winter. Recently, on one of those disgustingly beautiful mornings when it was cold but the sky was clear, the sun shone cheerfully and there was no wind at all, I went for a long run on the south shore of the lake.

As I ran along, suddenly the wind arrived, pushing at my back. It came roaring in, exactly at one o'clock, as if it was returning from a long lunchbreak. I turned, squinting my eyes to protect them from blowing beach sand, and saw clouds beginning to pile up and droop over our side of the Sierra crest.

It was winter.

The lake, moments before flat and blue, began to churn with waves and generate whitecaps. Tumbleweeds, the wandering skeletons of that non-native pest, Russian thistle, rolled past. Many lodged at the water's edge. I knew that if I returned the next day the tumbleweeds would be frosted white by salt spray. They always remind me of the tumbleweed snowmen which, every Christmas when I was growing up in the Mojave Desert, we made by piling three rounds on top of each other and coating them with that white "imitation snow" that comes in spray cans.

The waves were already generating soapsuds along the shore. The thick piles of white foam, a natural reaction when the lake's carbonate-rich water is agitated, would also decorate the shore the next morning. Have you ever seen frozen soapsuds? Yet another strange feature of this strange lake.

The wind blew hard that afternoon and all night. The next morning it stopped. But the clouds were here, finally, and snow began to sift down. And Mono Lake grew quiet.

There are kinds and degrees of quiet. Much of the winter Mono Lake is an exceptionally still place—when the wind is not blowing. It can come close to being totally silent ("quiet" and "silence" are, of course two different things). It is not because nothing moves or is alive in this winter landscape. Look closely and you will see plenty of tracks in the snow that show the area abounds with critters. But they are rabbits and hares, weasels and shrews, voles and mice—animals that specialize in quiet. They are the hunted and the hunters who never draw attention to themselves. Watch the sky and you will see more silent hunters: the hawks and eagles patrolling overhead.

Winter is the quiet season for our park operation too. In the list of "most-asked-questions" we rangers hear, is: "What do you do in the winter?" It is true that much of our job revolves around people, and fewer people are here in the winter. It is much quieter at Mono Lake right now than in summer, because we'll count about 4000 visitors in December, compared to almost 40,000 in August. So we cut back to a barebones staff. We plan exhibits and catch up on other projects which we were too busy to handle in the summer. And we enjoy the quiet.

We're still around to listen to those questions from the people who do come here, of course. Oddly, when the winter weather gets bad we often see *more* people at Mono Lake. If wind or heavy snow shuts the lifts down, skiers who cannot ski come our direction.

Of course, stormy days are full of noise and tumult. But when the skiing is good, things slow down for us again. And then, on those special winter days, we get the comments and questions about quiet. Snow carpets the ground and frosts the tufa formations. Ice crystals decorate the shrubs. Someone gets out of their car and, in a few moments, notices the conspicuous absence of sound. They approach and, in a hushed voice—as if they don't want to disturb the effect—say, "It's so wonderfully quiet here."

Absence of noise is a valuable treasure. It is one of Mono Lake's precious resources, worth protecting.

So enjoy the winter scene at the ski areas—the excitement and color and even the clamor and crowds. But if you need a change, come see Mono Lake.

Best wishes for the winter holidays, from the rangers of the Mono Lake Tufa State Reserve.

Happy quiet season!

# POGONIP

"**W**hat is it?!" he asked in a bewildered voice.

"Pogonip," was the mystifying reply, in a voice full of age and patience.

"It's so cold and dark," said the voice of the newcomer to the Mono Basin. "So foggy. I can't see. Why is it like this? Yesterday was clear and nice."

"It is pogonip. The freezing fog. The weatherman calls it that now, but it is a Paiute Indian word."

"It feels like 'white death' to me."

"Ah, yes. Its cold can be deadly. Its darkness too. When the fog comes and lingers, sometimes for days, maybe stretching to one or two weeks, then people may know gloom. Some despair of ever seeing the sun again."

"Who are you anyway? The fog makes it hard to see. You talk kind of funny."

"I am the mysterious voice that is answering your questions. I am supposed to sound like this."

"Oh. Of course. Then maybe you can answer another one: Will the fog hang around long this time? I mean my vacation lasts another week; the motel's already been paid. I don't think I could stand a whole week in this stuff."

"Pogonip is here only when snow blankets the land around Mono Lake, and only when the winter weather is clear and calm. You can always leave it, you know—just climb a few hundred feet uphill. The sun will break through and you will look out over cottony tops of white cloud filling the basin below. It is a beautiful sight."

"Yes, I would like to see that! It sounds like being in an airplane, looking down on top of clouds." But he grew more subdued, "Eventually I will have to return, to come back into the cold and dark of the fog. And you didn't really answer my question, you know, Mr. Mysterious Wise Voice. If I have to be under the fog, or inside it, like now, I'd like it to go away soon. Is it going to last my whole vacation?"

"Look around you now," the voice commanded. "Look closely at the trees and the bushes; look even at the ground. Have eyes that see! See how the fog and time have worked together to decorate the land. Pogonip brings its greatest beauty within the fog itself—for those who look closely enough."

He looked, then, and saw white frost on every tree branch and shrub, coating every surface. Even the ground, he saw, had a layer of loose ice crystals, inches deep.

"Why, it's a fairyland!" the visitor exclaimed. "Look at the crystals. It's...it's like everything's been frosted or—no, that's not right; not frosted, but decorated with tiny jewels. Not even that says it right. This is what Jack Frost is all about, but here he's covered *everything*!"

He heard a low chuckle. "Jack Frost? Perhaps. You begin to see. It—or he, if you like—does decorate everything; even *you*, if you would stand still long enough."

The newcomer turned, searching for the dark shape which had produced the mysterious voice from the fog. But the shape was lost in the gloom and the voice was coming from farther away.

"The longer the fog stays, the larger and longer grow the crystals. If you are lucky you may be given the privilege of seeing it at its best, when the fog lifts and the sun is allowed a few brief moments to play light-games with the crystals, before they melt away."

"That sounds really beautiful. Now where did I set my camera? Damn the fog! I mean—no, don't go telling me again; I know the fog does pretty things. But it's deathly cold. I wonder if my camera will even work at these temperatures."

"Not all the earth's beauty is gentle. Pogonip is cold, dark, and it makes those trapped beneath its fog blanket yearn for the sun. But for eyes that are open and see, it is also a gift of fäerie, decorating the land."

"Yes, but..."

"What more can I tell you?" asked the voice, wearily now, it seemed. It was moving farther and farther away, yet he still heard the words clearly.

"The answer to the question I asked before," he shouted. "When will it end?"

"When the weather gets bad," the voice answered. And then it was gone.

# Ouzel Omens

"Do you believe in signs?" The other man looked at Scott English, generally a sober, rational scientific sort of guy, as though he had flipped his lid. "Signs?"

The two men were working along Lee Vining Creek in late winter, selecting test sites for this year's revegetation efforts. It is all part of the court-mandated work to restore the creek to its "pre-diversion" conditions. Streams flowing to Mono Lake were never supposed to be totally dried up by the diversions to Los Angeles, according to Fish & Game law. So now the hard work is beginning to try to reestablish conditions in the creek and along its banks to restore high quality fish habitat.

Scott and his co-worker had been trying to decide if a certain site was suitable for planting, when Scott received the "sign." An ouzel landed in the middle of that part of the stream. A water ouzel. The first one they had seen along lower Lee Vining Creek. Perhaps a "sign" that the study plot there was well chosen.

The ouzel was definitely a sign of change, anyway. Lee Vining Creek, along with Parker, Walker and lower Rush Creeks, was dead-dry most of the last 50 years. Ouzels live along water—in the water, much of the time. They are plump, gray little birds that some people call "dippers" because they constantly bob up and down, whether standing still or walking. They can "fly" submerged, searching for water insects to eat.

John Muir, in *The Mountains of California*, called the ouzel "...the mountain streams' own darling, the hummingbird of blooming waters, loving rocky ripple slopes and sheets of foam as a bee loves flowers, as a lark loves sunshine and meadows. Among all the mountain birds, none has cheered me so much in my lonely wanderings." Muir particularly loved their songs.

I don't know if Scott English had Muir's writing in mind when he saw that ouzel in Lee Vining Creek. But I do know that Scott has been noting each return of a water-loving creature to that area. There's a kingfisher hanging out near the county road crossing now. And a great blue heron. Fish-eaters.

In the stream itself you can discover fish food. Caddis fly larvae and stone fly larvae are back among the rocks. Trout love them. Where vegetation has returned to the shore, this summer you should be able to find the cellophane-like, skeletal shells of the larvae left behind on stems when the larvae emerge as flying adults.

Some plants have begun to grow again along the channel. Tiny little cottonwood trees are sprouting here and there. Last spring an amazing display of blue lupine flowers appeared near the Lee Vining Creek crossing of the county road. The seeds must have been waiting there in the soil for years.

Water brings the return of life.

But despite these hopeful signs, the flowing water may not, in itself, restore the old conditions to the creek channel. Unfortunately, after all the streamside vegetation had been long dead, a couple times over the years high-water floods scoured the unstabilized channel, altering its bed and its very location.

A healthy stream needs a variety of riffles and deep pools, quiet and swift water, gravels for spawning and places for trout to escape and hide. And it needs banks stabilized by grasses, shrubs and trees.

Cottonwoods, aspens, and willows will have other benefits, of course. They will shade the stream in places. They will die, over time, their branches and trunks falling into the stream, causing new pools to form behind them and providing new places for trout to hide. And the trees will become habitat for land dwellers. Places for kingfishers and bald eagles to perch. Nesting sites. Homes for insects and reptiles and mammals.

The green strip of riparian vegetation that lines water courses is also attractive to human mammals. As the creeks recover they will once again be wonderful places to hike, picnic, and yes, even to fish. The creek corridor will be an oasis in the arid Mono Basin.

Scott English is part of the "ground crew" that will help this to happen in our lifetimes. His work reminds me of a computer game I recently bought. It's one of those mazes with 20 levels of hazards and rewards. A horribly addictive game. I love the problem-solving, but imagine the horror of reaching level 19, surviving all those hazards, and then making one deadly mistake. Do I have to start all over again from Level 1, go all the way through the entire game once more in order to make new progress toward that ultimate Crown of Kroz?

No, thank goodness. Not if I use the "restore" function. If I am wise, I'll have taken steps so the computer memory starts me off again at a higher level. By restoring to that point I can shortcut the long, long process of beginning over from scratch.

The court has mandated that the once-dry creeks flowing to Mono Lake be restored. And we aren't going to have to wait for 40 or 60 or 100 years to see if it can ever successfully be done. Efforts are beginning now to actively restore the streams.

The ouzel and the other water creatures show that the process is underway. Stream-channel work and planting of riparian vegetation will speed things along.

The next few years should bring wonderful changes to the streams flowing into Mono Lake. The ouzels are back. You're welcome too.

# SOME WINTER VOICES

 *"W*e've driven by Mono Lake a million times, but we had no idea it was so special until today."

During the past ten years that I have worked at the Mono Lake Tufa State Reserve, I have heard that statement, or something similar, hundreds of times. It usually comes from a visitor who has finally left the highway and driven the few miles to the South Tufa Area. We are in the business of changing a lot of preconceived notions about this place.

Before coming here, many people might have no opinion at all about the lake. Afterwards, they seem to always go away with strong opinions, mostly positive, rarely negative.

We pay a lot of attention to those comments and opinions. Some are gathered firsthand, but also in the thousands of written comments left behind on visitor register pages. The comments are worth reviewing. Some of them are humorous; some offer helpful suggestions; all are revealing.

Right up front I have to say that the vast majority of them are similar to this: *"Save It !"* Or this: *"Stop L.A.!"* (I ought to point out that our visitor registers don't solicit "water issue" comments, per se. They just have a place for "Comments/Suggestions," along with name, date, number in party and hometown.) I actually don't think even the Los Angeles Dept. of Water & Power would find this too surprising. There's a lot of public awareness out there about Mono Lake's water problems. Visitors to the lake seem to like to express themselves, especially after seeing firsthand what's at stake. Anyway, just remember that those are the vast majority of comments written, because I'm not going to say more about them. We're going to look at some "not so common" reactions from this winter.

*"An eerie, desolate mecca of life that once was."* Hmmm. That was written by someone from Martinez on 1/8/90. The only problem with that poetic statement is that it sounds like the place is dead. Of course, in January it can come close to looking that way, to a casual observer. And the tufa towers often impress people with that kind of moody speculation about how things used to be. I just hope that person returns next summer when the lake is teeming with animal life all over its surface and especially under the water. Mono Lake is not a dead sea. Not as of now, anyway.

*"Looked better in the postcards."* This writer was at the Old Marina site on 1/9/90. We try, with signs and exhibits, to tell those people who pull off Highway 395 where the lake is closest to the highway, that they have not yet made it to the real beauty spots. The Old Marina is okay, but photographers seldom take postcard pictures there. I hope that particular visitor makes it to the South Tufa Area soon, or one of the more remote, incredible spots waiting to be found. Then they might go away agreeing with the visitor from Poland who wrote, *"An awesome display of nature's creativity,"* or the one from Los Angeles who said, *"Unique—from a world traveler,"* or the West German: *"Discovered a new planet."* (12/20, 12/22, 12/29/89)

Here's an interesting series of comments that were left recently:

"*Came around the corner and there it was. Wow !*" (Durban, South Africa)

"*Best surprise of trip.*" (Kirkland, Washington)

"*Ugly, useless—waste.*" (Fresno, CA) [Well, look who's talking. Sorry, I couldn't resist that stab at the nice valley town of Fresno. Actually, this was another Old Marina comment; not all of the comments there are so negative, by the way.]

"*Es ist schöo.*" (Switzerland) [I don't speak the language, but I think they liked the place.]

"*A white weasel !*" (San Francisco) [Lucky people; walk the Reserve's boardwalk to the shoreline below the Mono Lake County Park and you might see the critter in his winter coat too.]

"*Fantastic and imaginative. Greater than Disneyland, says Alex, age 4 and a half.*" (Fremont, CA) [That parent is raising a natural-born ranger.]

As the years have passed we have collected a lot of visitor register pages. For example, 192,000 visitors—give or take a few thousand—came to Mono Lake in 1989. Most of them came in parties of 3, and about one-third of those parties bothered to sign our registers (yes, we've actually counted.) So last year we collected around 21,000 signatures, on over 800 pages. We've been doing that for long enough that it's getting to be a storage problem.

With so much data to analyze, it is not surprising that some patterns have appeared. Some rather odd patterns, actually. See what you make of these (a small sample within the last month; and no, I'm not making this stuff up):

"*Very sexy place.*" (Pacific Palisades)

"*Great for newlyweds.*" (Chino, CA)

"*Erotic environment.*" (Palos Verdes)

"*Made us horny.*" (Haifa, Israel)

"*It was not a good place for making love.*" (No town listed) [We never said it was, after all. Still, something about the place must have put it into their minds.]

It would be safest to make no comment about those comments. I'll only say that they are a regular occurrence on the registers. And remind you all: Smokey's Watching!

Voices. So many hundreds of thousands of human voices. All talking about the impressions left by Mono Lake. Impressions gathered, sometimes, in a quick stop of less than fifteen minutes. Sometimes from just a view out a car window. But, happily, more and more often during a close-up look at what Mono Lake has to offer.

If only the silent "voices" of 4 trillion brine shrimp, the raucous screams of 50,000 gulls and their 25,000 chicks, the quiet buzz of zillions (a whole lot, anyway) of alkali flies, the soft "plops" of 800,000 diving eared grebes, and the whir of 140,000 phalarope wings in flight, can somehow be effectively added to all those human voices, talking about Mono Lake.

# In Search of
# Happily Ever After

# DRAIN IT AND PAVE IT

 Believe it or not, once in awhile some-
one suggests that the best thing to do
with Mono Lake would be to drain it
and pave it over. Think of the benefits, they have been
known to say, of so much parking space, room for
skateboard rinks and basketball courts... After all, what
good, really, is that kind of salty lake?

Those people aren't really serious, of course. They are
just testing for a reaction. But I have also noticed that the
ones who are willing to make such suggestions have usually never been to Mono Lake. Oh, they may have *seen* the
lake many times as they drove by on Highway 395. But I
don't hear that kind of talk from people who have actually
stopped and spent some time. Most of those real visitors to
Mono Lake come away with plenty of personal reasons to
value this place.

This overheard conversation gave me a whole new
perspective on this issue:

"Drain it and pave it? Are you crazy? You want to bring
economic collapse to the western hemisphere, promote
criminal behavior and, worst of all, ruin your sex life?"

"What are you talking about? What has Mono Lake got to do with any of that...especially my sex life?"

"Ah, clearly you haven't given this enough thought. Listen and heed: First, consider the consequences should the lake dry up. (I will postpone consideration of the paving question for a few moments). Without the water of Mono Lake, with its unique chemical conditions, the brine shrimp and alkali flies would die. Millions of millions of lives would be lost...tiny ones, to be sure, but life nonetheless. Without the shrimp and flies, over a million birds would no longer be able to feed here. Without—"

"Yes, yes. I see the point. What if I say I don't care, huh?"

"Please, let me finish. You don't see *anything* yet. You're future happiness is in great jeopardy. Remember, your—"

"Sex life? Right. Sure. This is crazy, but go ahead."

"So. If 800,000 eared grebes and 140,000 phalaropes were no longer supported by Mono Lake, they might never make it to winter ranges in South and Central America. And without all that bird life down there, the predators which feed on the birds would decline. With the decline in hawks and foxes would follow an increase in rodents, which are also controlled by the same predators. Thus, rodents would overrun farms, producing famine. Also, insects normally fed on by the grebes and phalaropes would increase. Such insects could be disease vectors. The miserable humans affected by all this would flee northward, flooding cities with immigrants. Disease, famine, overcrowding...can crime not follow? Can economies stand under such an onslaught? Can—"

"Can I stand here and listen to this nonsense any longer?"

"You're sitting. Don't forget about your sex life."

"Yeah, cut to the important stuff."

"But we still haven't dealt with the paving idea. Consider. Mono Lake covers sixty square miles. If you pave that much land there may not be enough asphalt left to maintain our highways. Yet gas guzzling machines of every sort will be attracted to the area. Smog, congestion, and noise will cover the hot baking surface of pavement during the summer months. The heat will be so intense that airplanes flying overhead will be buffeted by the rising heat columns. Commercial flights will be forced to circle around the basin to avoid the turbulence. Of course, the desperate, starving folks from down south will be having their effect on this area too. Pollution, crime, ugliness..."

"Enough, already. You forced me to listen to all this because of one very personal effect you predicted for me. Are you ever going to explain about my sex life?"

"Oh, that. Yes. Well. You should realize that those people who really know and love Mono Lake would find it very hard to sit still and accept all of this. Since *I* love *you*, I want you to know that if you don't wise up, get out there, and see for yourself what it is you so casually talk about destroying, then I will personally see to it that your future sex life will be as barren as that bleak, asphalt basin would become. Understand...honey?"

And then she dragged him by his ear out of his comfortable seat (in a motorhome with a satellite dish on the roof), away from his football game on the little portable television, and marched him down the South Tufa trail.

# MONEY TALK$

 "There're no fish in this lake, are there?"

Oh boy, he thought. Here we go again. "No, ma'am. No fish. But—"

"And I notice there're no motor boats on the lake. Do people *do* anything with this lake?"

Yep, one of those. "Well, about 200,000 people come to Mono Lake to walk the shore and look at things every year. Most—"

"Sure, but...I mean, is there anything *useful* about it?"

"There is a commercial harvest of brine shrimp. They freeze dry them as food for tropical fish."  Ah, the word "commercial" always gets their attention, he thought. Now, if she'll let me finish a sentence, maybe I can open up her mind to—

But he didn't even finish the thought before she began speaking again. "So that must be why all the fuss. There had to be *something* of value here."  She punctuated that statement with a look around and a face which showed that she was having trouble seeing anything worthwhile in the nearby view.

"Have you been to the south shore of the lake?" Ah ha! Ask her a question; that'll capture her attention.

But she began backing away, wary of being trapped into an extended conversation. "No. No, we're just passing by. Maybe some other time. We just have time for a quick stop. Thank you. Goodbye now."

"But..." Sigh. I wanted you to go see some of the incredible beauty of the south shore, he thought, watching her drive away. To walk among the tufa towers and see the views of the Sierra and volcanic craters ringing the massive azure lake. And to see some of the many living creatures supported by Mono Lake—the trillions of brine shrimp and alkali flies that feed over a million birds—mostly gulls, grebes and shorebirds.

Sure, there's no fish. And most of the birds are non-game species. I just wanted you to take a little more time and a little closer look, because I know that people who do usually go away in awe at the scenery. I realize that many sense they are outsiders here; no human invented the ancient, balanced, living ecosystem of Mono Lake. Maybe you would have been surprised, like most other people who get a glimpse of all that, to discover yourself caring about Mono Lake's preservation, hoping it will always be there, alive and well for you to visit the next time you travel this way. Even if you can't imagine any way for people to make money out of the place.

Sigh.

*****

## A Humanities Test

A. A steep-walled valley or canyon with a river running through it (Yosemite Valley, for example) is good for:

    a. A water-storage reservoir (see "H," below)

    b. A hydroelectric generating reservoir

    c. Spanning with engineering marvels called bridges

    d. ?

B. A flower is good for:
   a. Producing perfumes for scenting human females
   b. Reproducing certain plants of economic value
   c. Smelling, unless you have allergies.
   e. ?

C. An ancient forest is good for:
   a. Lumber
   b. The tourist industry, if adequate roads are built
      and a drive-through tree is provided
   c . Adding the words "overmature" and "senescence" to
      some foresters' vocabularies
   d. ?

D. A fur bearing mammal is good for:
   a. Turning into a fur coat
   b. Keeping ancient trapping skills of our ancestors
      alive for future generations
   c. Nothing, if it's a skunk
   d. Not much, if it's a coyote
   e. ?

E. Birds are good for something if they are:
   a. Waterfowl
   b. Upland game fowl
   c. Have pretty feathers
   d. Sing pretty songs
   e. ?

F. Flies are good for:
   a. Catching trout
   b. ?

G. Brine shrimp are good for:

a. Feeding tropical fish
b. A food source for some birds (but see "E" above to see if those kind of birds are worth the trouble)
c. ?

H. Lakes are good so long as you can:
   a. Fish
   b. Water ski
   c. Ship the water in them to some urban area
   d. Build a resort on their shoreline
   e. Figure out some other way to make money out of them
   f. ?

I. Humans are good for:
   a. Reproducing humans
   b. Building cities
   c. ?

Sigh.

# IN SEARCH OF HAPPILY EVER AFTER

NOTICE: Persons attempting to find a motive in this narrative may well discover one, or even two; persons attempting to find a moral in it will (hopefully) succeed; persons attempting to find a plot may, alas, seek in vain. Herein is a story of herdsmen that has almost nothing to do with 4-legged beasts, really. I confess, 'tis a parable, and therefore hopes to sway your mind about *humans*. It is a story built on high hopes. Beware.

The Author (with a cordial bow to Mark Twain)

\*\*\*\*\*

*Once upon a time in a far distant land there was a pasture, open to all the people. Each herdsman and herdswoman (this was an enlightened pastoral society) grazed as many cattle on that common pasture as they could.*

*For centuries this worked just fine. Wars, famine, disease, and even cattle rustlers kept the numbers of cattle and people below the natural limits of that land.*

*But, inevitably, it seems, a day came when social progress improved the general health of the population so that more children lived to adulthood and more adults lived to ripe old age. And thus, a great tragedy came to pass.*

("The Tragedy of the Commons." That phrase stuck in my head, perhaps better than any other I learned twenty years ago at the university. It kept recurring to me in recent years, until I finally dug out the old reference. Garrett Hardin, of U.C. Santa Barbara was the author, in *Science* magazine, way back in 1968.)

*You see, throughout history each herder put as many cattle as they could on their common pasture. But the human population had now grown to the point that the pasture was approaching its limit for cows.*

*The people were well aware, of course, that there were more and more cows out there. They could see them crowding for elbow-room* (elbows? why not?), *and hear them and smell them; especially the sound and odor were becoming more and more a background factor in their lives. Most of them recognized that there was only so much space available, let alone grass sufficient to feed each cow. They saw the crunch coming, yet, unfortunately, each of them was a rational being.*

*That was unfortunate because, as rational herders, each went through—consciously or unconsciously—the following calculation: a)If I add one more cow to the common herd, I receive all of the value of that animal when it is sold: positive benefit to me = +1; but b) another cow will hurt the pasture, hindering my cow's growth a bit, yet that effect on the pasture will be averaged out among all the cows: negative effect to me = a tiny fraction of -1. Conclusion: the only sensible thing to do is add that cow to the herd.*

*The herders were sensible and rational. All of them kept adding cows. Eventually all of the cattle began to weaken. And inevitably, the grass in the pasture was all gone early one summer. The cattle died.*

*Then the ancient, harsh means of controlling the human population—famine and disease—began to once again do for the people what they had not done for themselves. The people began dying too.*

*One herder said, "We should have restricted the number of cows, my friends. And had fewer babies ourselves."*

*But objections were, even then, voiced. The gist of them seemed to be: "This is a free society. Nobody's going to tell us we can't raise as many cows as we want, like our parents and grandparents could. It's always been that way. And as for babies, you better just back off. Hear?"*

*The herder said,* (unknowingly echoing the words of Dr. Hardin), *"But unrestrained freedom in the commons is what brought ruin to us all."*

("Mutual coercion, mutually agreed upon." That's the other phrase that stuck in my head all these years. That phrase was Dr. Hardin's prescription for avoiding this tragedy. But has it ever been a realistic answer? I wonder. What if there *is* no mutual agreement? Anyway, in this fable, none of the herders brought up the phrase.)

*It was too late for those poor people. They had no choice but to stop arguing, pack up and move on—those that still had the strength—searching for some other pasture where they could start over.*

*That was an ancient pattern, too. Moving on, generally moving west, when things got tight.*

*But it didn't work this time.*

*It seems the human population had been succeeding, and there-fore growing, all over the land. There were other pastures, but every one of them was either at, or fast approaching, its own limit of cows and people.*

*Little in the long history of these people had prepared them for life in an era of limits. Change was not easy for them. And so they suffered the ultimate tragedy: their once-upon-a-time story had no happy ending.*

Perhaps this concept has been dredged from my memory because Mono Lake, where I work, is a perfect example of the tragedy of the commons. The cumulative effect of in-dividual daily decisions about water threatens to kill the lake. Each gallon wasted or saved by me or you seems inconsequential in the big picture, yet multiplied by millions can have amazing and tragic consequences.

But Mono Lake also offers an example of hope. Unlike those herders, our society has something called a "public trust doctrine" that may be the means to save the lake. Everyone may not be free to use water without constraint— and that's hard for some people to face—but it can be a way to coerce the stubborn ones, the selfish ones, to cooperate for a greater good.

No, not exactly "mutual agreement mutually agreed upon." Environmental issues often are not resolved so amicably, unfortunately. Another bit of ancient university trivia suggests why:

*An experimenter at Harvard once connected a cat's hearing nerve to a scope and then sounded sharp clicks in the cat's ear. The scope registered the vibrations. But when a jar with white mice was placed in front of the cat, it not only ignored the clicks, but the needle failed to move. This was astonishing. Even if the cat was too fascinated by the mice to pay attention to the sound, the impulse should still have travelled from its eardrum to the scope. Somehow the cat, focusing on its "bread and butter" stimulus, completely cut off the "extraneous" noise.*

Do you wonder, like me, why reasoned debate and seemingly compelling arguments so seldom alter people's opinions? Perhaps we, like the cat, have a cut-off mechanism that keeps us from hearing each other at all when the argument is distracting us from—or conflicting with—our personal "bread and butter" concerns.

Yet this concept seems so important that I want to try. We share so many threatened "commons"—threatened because the level of our "sharing" has reached critical limits. Examples are found wherever individuals are faced with that equation—balancing personal benefits against widely-shared costs. And wherever they make the rational, though short-sighted, choice.

Think about our cars. Each one, by itself, is a technological blessing. It is the solution to our individual transportation needs. It is only because millions of them are on the road that every car has become a poisoner of the common air and congester of the common freeways. (If you've driven in Southern California recently you know what "saturation" is all about when it comes to roadways, and you know what it is to waste major chunks of your life in traffic jams.)

But ultimately all "commons" issues come down to one overriding conflict: a burgeoning human population versus a planet of finite resources. There *are* limits. We can grow until they are reached, or passed, or we can face the truth and seek ways to avoid tragedy.

Personally, I prefer stories with happy endings.

# TEN YEARS LATER

There is a scrapbook in the office of the Mono Lake Tufa State Reserve which is labeled "Unit History—Vol. I." The first entry is dated January 1, 1982.

Ten years ago, this New Years Day, the Reserve was created. Ten years. Amazing. New Years and anniversary celebrations were invented so we might stir out of our daily routines and look at just how far we have come. So, with your indulgence, I would like to share some other entries from that unit history (which now fills three thick binders).

*"April 15, 1982—Ranger staff reports to Mono Lake."* That refers to my wife, Janet, and me, who have together served as the unit ranger for the Reserve. It's a job-sharing arrangement that was a "first" for the State Park System. It has been a successful experiment for us, our supervisors, and for Nick and Ryan, our sons, now 9 and 6.

*"July 14, 1982—Finally got an office telephone !"* Note the gap between April and July. The "!" says it all. That year was not unlike this one in some ways; money in the State budget was so tight that purchase and hookup of a telephone had to wait until the start of a new fiscal year. At

least we did have more money for seasonal help back then. Ranger Leslie Dawson started working with us on July 6, 1982. Leslie now teaches 7th and 8th grade at Mammoth High School, but she labored mightily and enthusiastically for three seasons to help get the Reserve established. We still miss her. (Not that we could afford to pay her salary these days after years of budget cuts. Now we hire student interns and one paid park aid, David Marquart, who has dedicated 9 summers to the Reserve.)

Public tours were instituted that first summer, and they have continued every weekend throughout the entire span of years—daily, of course, in the summer. We estimate that our own staff have guided over 35,000 visitors on 1600 tours of the lakeshore by now. That doesn't include tours also offered by the Forest Service and the Mono Lake Committee.

That first year we also installed temporary exhibits and removed literally tons of trash from the lakeshore—everything from old TVs to several miles of detonating wire left by the military at "Navy Beach" in the early '60s.

*"Dec. 25, 1982—Nicholas Carle is born !"* (Now you see why I asked for your indulgence. This has been a personal, as well as official, history for the Carle family. Kids were a major part of the justification for this whole job-sharing arrangement, after all.)

*"April 1, 1983—Negit Island landbridge is re-flooded."* Remember the winter of...? What a classic phrase; makes me feel like an old-timer for sure. But *do* you remember that winter of 82/83? The heaviest Sierran snowpack in 100 years of recordkeeping. Janet and I came to Mono Lake expecting to watch the water decline, as it had been so steadily doing, yet the lake rose several feet that winter and continued to rise for the next four years.

*"May 1983—This month 12 school groups visited the Reserve."* There's a pattern that has not changed. May is school group month. They keep us busy, drive us crazy, and make our job very fulfilling.

*"June 30, 1983—Tioga Pass finally opened."*

The rest of that second year saw permanent exhibits installed in display shelters around the lake. On October 28 we installed the "Mark Twain Scenic Tufa Trail" panels at the South Tufa area. Most visitors never see a ranger at the lake; we had spent a big part of the prior winter writing the text and designing the layout for this self-guided trail. It is one of our accomplishments which I remain most proud of.

*"Apr. 4, 1984—Kellogg films a TV commercial for 'C3PO' cereal at South Tufa, complete with tufa monsters and fake towers."* Even R2D2 and C3PO, the Star Wars robots, were there, along with a 50 person film crew and lots of headaches for our staff. Somehow we, and the resource, survived the "entertaining" ordeal. TV, film, music video, and magazine ads still provide us the occasional challenge.

*"Apr. 13, 1984—First 600 feet of boardwalk were constructed across the marsh below the County Park."* Little did we know what we were starting. This boardwalk has been extended again and again, with lots of volunteer help from the Eastern Sierra Audubon Society and other local friends. You can now walk over a half-mile of redwood planks to view the marsh and reach the still-retreating lakeshore.

*"Oct. 22, 1984—Tamarisk removal project begins."* Another, "little did we know" story. This non-native, water-sucking pest of a shrub has proven widespread and persistent. The fight goes on.

*"Nov. 1984—The Mono Basin National Forest Scenic Area is created."* Shortly thereafter our two agencies signed a joint operating agreement, recognizing that our responsibilities and jurisdiction overlap. It has worked remarkably well. In December, 1991 the Reserve office moved into the new Scenic Area Visitor Center building.

*"Apr. 6, 1985—A pair of osprey take up residence on a tufa tower offshore from Navy Beach."* They were the first osprey, a large fish-eating hawk, to nest in Mono County in 20 years. But they would not successfully raise any chicks until 1989 (two), 1990 (one), and 1991 (two).

*"Apr. 19, 1985—Ryan Carle is born !"* Yes, job-sharing was working just fine.

*"June 24-28, 1985—Junior Ranger program has 15 kids."* We have offered this five day activity through the Mammoth Elementary School summer program almost every year, watching a generation of Mammoth Lakes kids grow up.

I'd better start condensing or I'll never get through the next six years. Some things have become annual traditions. Fourth of July parades in Mammoth and Bridgeport always have their "walking, talking tufa towers." The first Halloween Moonlight Walk was on October 27, 1985. This year, the 6th for this "scary" event, over 110 people attended, but the courage awards go to the 50 hardy souls who showed up in 1990 when the temperature was 15 degrees and it was windy. We sponsored photo workshops for quite a few years, until they became so popular that other groups filled the need.

The years have brought research permits to monitor, off-road violations, gull censuses, vegetation monitoring, livestock trespass issues—the varied range of duties that all fall within a ranger's scope. Visitation jumped from 107,000 in 1983 (our first full year of counting) to 192,000 by 1989—a total of one and a half million people in ten years!

*"June 15, 1987—Got a copy machine !"* Some things seem basic, but take time.

*"Jan 23, 1988—Memorial Service for David Gaines; 320 people at the South Tufa Area."* We miss you, Dave. He was a founder of the Mono Lake Committee and one of the strongest supporters of the Reserve.

*"Sept. 16, 1990—A second boardwalk is constructed across marsh at the Old Marina site, dedicated to the memory of David Gaines."* Now wheelchairs can reach the lakeshore.

Well, I'm skipping lots of stuff now. Another major highlight for me has been the schedule of star talks we've offered every single summer. The lakeshore is a fantastic place to lie back and become lost in the universe. We spend many hours in our office, preparing comments on planning documents and EIRs relative to Mono Lake. We've spent some time in court too, adding our particular perspective to the water issues here. Janet developed training programs attended each June by interpreters from Yosemite National Park and the local Forest Service Districts. I've taught CPR and first aid in the local community and for the search and rescue team.

The latest entry in the unit history reads:  "January 1, 1992—Tenth Anniversary of the Reserve!  Also Janet and Dave Carle's 15th Wedding Anniversary."  Our youngest son is already 6 and a half, going on 7.

And the Mono Lake Tufa State Reserve is 10, going on forever.

# ARTEMISIA PRESS BOOKS

**Distributional Checklist of N. American Birds**          $15.00
David DeSante and Peter Pyle

**The Distribution of the Birds of California**          hard $25.00
Joseph Grinnell and Alden H. Miller          paper  $18.00

**Birds of Yosemite and the East Slope**          $15.00
David Gaines

**Paiute, Prospector, Pioneer:  The Bodie-**          $9.50
**Mono Lake Area in the Nineteenth Century.**
Thomas C. Fletcher

**Pioneers of the Mono Basin**          $7.95
 Margaret Calhoun

**Quaternary History of the Mono Valley**          $9.95
Israel C. Russell

**Mono Lake Viewpoint**          $5.95
David Carle

**********************************************************************

California residents please add 7.25% tax.  Book rate shipping included in price. Artemisia Press, P.O. Box 119, Lee Vining, CA 93541 (619) 647-6496. Dealer inquiries welcome.